D1648904

The March of the Montana Column

THE MARCH OF THE

A Prelude to the Custer Disaster

MONTANA COLUMN

by Lieutenant James H. Bradley

Edited by Edgar I. Stewart

Foreword by Paul L. Hedren

NORMAN AND LONDON
UNIVERSITY OF OKLAHOMA PRESS

To the Members of the Staff
of the Historical Society of Montana,
both past and present, in grateful appreciation

Library of Congress Catalog Card Number: 61–6494
ISBN: 0–8061–2316–8

New edition copyright © 1961 by the University of Oklahoma Press,
Publishing Division of the University. All rights reserved. Manufac-
tured in the U.S.A. First printing, 1961. First paperback printing,
1991.

Contents

Illustrations

Foreword
by Paul L. Hedren

THE BRADLEY JOURNAL! Scholars working the endlessly fertile fields of the Great Sioux War of 1876–77 know instantly First Lieutenant James Howard Bradley's classic account of Colonel John Gibbon's infantry campaign. Researchers know, too, the poignant story behind the abrupt ending of the narrative.

Transforming his field diary into a polished journal, Bradley had finished his rewrite through June 26, 1876. Recounting Crow Indian reports about Custer's demise just received by Gibbon and General Alfred Terry, his final entry notes the apprehension that filled the army camp.

We know that on the morrow, June 27, Bradley and his Indian scouts would discover Custer's dead on the east banks of the Little Bighorn. But in mid-1877, before Bradley could outline this horror, he was called with his regiment, the Seventh U.S. Infantry, to campaign against the Nez Perce Indians, who were fleeing their Oregon homeland bound for Canada. At the Battle of the Big Hole, Montana, on August 9, 1877, the thirty-three-year-old husband, father, and budding scholar was killed in the opening moments of that fight.

Had James Bradley lived, he might figure more prominently among that small corps of inquisitive army officers, such men as John G. Bourke, Washington Matthews, Charles King, and Hiram M. Chittenden, who had insatiable appetites for the history and ethnohistory of the American West. Bradley's penchant becomes abundantly clear when one scans the calendar of his papers in the archives of the Montana Historical Society. There, in dozens of files, one sees the young officer's preliminary successes in collecting Montana territorial narratives. He was particularly fascinated by the fur trade of the early and mid-nineteenth century, and he is among the earliest to record accounts of Fort Benton and American Fur Company history in the Upper Missouri country. Despite having been slain so early in life, Bradley is memorialized today as one of Montana's great literary pioneers.

Similarly, Bradley's 1876 Sioux War journal ranks among the finest primary accounts of a conflict that pitted the U.S. army against Sioux and Cheyenne Indians as Euroamericans wrested new lands for mining, cattle, and settlement. Chief of scouts for John Gibbon's "Montana Column," Bradley filled his journal with trenchant, sometimes humorous, insights into the management and day-to-day operation of a small infantry and cavalry corps. His is a sensitive narrative, too. As tension grew on June 26—the troops were anticipating "one of the biggest Indian battles ever fought on this continent"—Bradley confides, "There is not much glory in Indian wars, but it will be worthwhile to have been present at such an affair as this."

These particular soldiers, of course, never participated in

this "biggest battle," but Bradley was positioned to receive the ominous initial reports of Custer's death and then to lead the combined Dakota and Montana column up the Little Bighorn and onto the Custer battlefield. At this late stage, Bradley's narrative, which never lacks freshness and vitality, becomes positively gripping. One must regret that it ends so abruptly.

On a recent visit to Helena, Montana, I had the pleasure of viewing Lieutenant Bradley's original manuscript journal. A substantial sheaf of loose papers, the journal has been a treasured possession of the Montana Historical Society since 1881. As I surveyed the working draft of what was becoming Bradley's wartime reminiscences, I was immediately impressed by the manuscript's physical characteristics. A few introductory sheets 8½ by 11 inches in size and labeled "Preface" were followed by another 135 leaves of a legal-size, cream-colored cotton rag paper. Many corners were frayed. Bradley hand worked both sides of each neatly ruled sheet, and then numbered each page to 269. Filed with the manuscript was an additional legal-size sheet, no doubt the lieutenant's cover, bearing the title "Journal of the Sioux Campaign on the Yellowstone in 1876; With Historical Sketches of the Country Traversed, and Outline Histories of the Sioux and Crow Indian Tribes."

Evidently Bradley crafted his Sioux War narrative from a more cryptic diary that his modern editor, Edgar Stewart, calls "rough field notes." This 1876 component apparently does not survive. Bradley enriched his narrative with carefully written accounts of the exploration, early occupation, and people of the Yellowstone River valley. To a Sioux War historian this original surviving journal is a piece of the "true cross."

Colonel Gibbon lamented the untimely death of his versatile subaltern. With the colonel's encouragement, Mary Bradley, the lieutenant's young widow, donated the journal and the remainder of her husband's papers to the Montana Historical Society in 1881. In 1896 the Sioux War journal was published in volume 2 of *Contributions to the Historical Society of Montana*, a volume that enjoyed only limited circulation. Subsequently, Edgar I. Stewart, among the most prolific scholars of Custer and the Little Bighorn and author of the timeless *Custer's Luck* (University of Oklahoma Press, 1955), added a new introduction to the 1896 printing, and the result was published by the University of Oklahoma Press in 1961. In recent years, copies of this edition likewise have become difficult to locate. James Bradley's *March of the Montana Column* remains one of the truly satisfying chronicles of the Great Sioux War of 1876–77, and this new, paperback edition is wholly welcome.

Introduction

IN THE ENORMOUS LITERATURE dealing with the Battle of the Little Big Horn River, generally known in history as "Custer's Last Stand," at least one item has failed to receive the attention that it deserves. This is the Journal kept by Lieutenant James H. Bradley of the Seventh Infantry, which records in considerable detail the major incidents of the march of the Montana Column, under the command of Colonel John Gibbon, from Fort Shaw and Fort Ellis to participate in the Sioux campaign of 1876. The Journal begins on the seventeenth of March, when five companies of the regiment marched from Fort Shaw. It ends abruptly with the entry for the twenty-sixth of June, when Colonel Gibbon's command camped on the site of present Crow Agency, Montana, amid abundant indications that the Seventh Cavalry had met with disaster. The abrupt ending was due to the fact that Lieutenant Bradley kept his record in the form of rough field notes and after his return to Fort Shaw in the fall of 1876 revised and rewrote the notes into more finished form. From these literary labors he was called by another Indian campaign, against Chief Joseph of the Nez Percés, from which he never returned being killed in action at the Battle of the Big Hole, so that his Journal remained uncompleted. In order to complete the account and not leave an unfinished story, a letter written by Lieutenant Bradley describing the finding of the bodies of Custer's command, is appended to the Journal. This provides a satisfactory conclusion to his account of the march of the Montana Column, although it is to be regretted that the Lieutenant was not allowed to complete the narration of the subsequent movements of Gibbon's command.

To the government of the United States, the Sioux Indians and, to a lesser extent, the Northern Cheyennes had been a perpetual and persistent source of trouble for more than a decade. And it should be emphasized in passing that the wrong was not all on one side and the right on the other. But this is not the place even to attempt to review the events of the tragic decade between the close of the Civil War and the disaster on the Little Big Horn. It is sufficient to note that it was a period in which the Indian Bureau tried, without success, to carry water on both shoulders, and in which the responsible officials of the government alternated between trying to pacify the Indians by a policy of sweet reasonableness and by one of beating them to death with a club. The trouble was that neither policy was continued long enough to have any chance of being effective, and by the year 1875, for a whole complex of reasons, the situation had become intolerable. Then the Indian Bureau, apparently as the only way out of a very unpleasant situation, resorted to drastic measures and ordered all Indians absent from their agencies to be back on the reservations by the first of February, 1876. That the order was in direct violation of a solemn treaty with the Sioux apparently bothered the Bureau not at all. Failure to comply with the order would be considered an act of defiance, and troops would be sent against the recalcitrant tribesmen.

The first of February came and went; the hostiles had showed no intention of complying with the order. The winter of 1875–76 was an exceptionally severe one; deep snows and sub-zero temperatures might have been cited in justifying the failure of the Indians to come in as ordered, but their failure was not due to the inclemency of the weather so much as to the fact that from experience the Indians simply did not believe that the order meant what it said. This time, however, they were to find that the government meant business, for, although apparently with some reluctance, the Indian Bureau carried out its threat and turned the recalcitrant bands over to the War Department for whatever action might be necessary.

Regardless of what the individual soldiers might feel, and there were many, including General Custer, who felt a strong bond of sympathy with the Indians, the official attitude toward the approaching hostilities was one of enthusiasm. The army had endured humiliation and insult at the hands of these same Indians for too long, without being allowed to strike back, not to have felt a sense of elation at an opportunity to even the score. Now was the time of reckoning, and the army intended to take full advantage of it.

The plan of operations was simplicity itself. According to the official estimates the wild bands did not number more than a few hundred at the most, and it was believed that a winter campaign would prove most effective, that the Indians could be chased back to their agencies and the troops could be back at their regular stations before the grass was well up in the spring. Since the hostile tribesmen were believed to be somewhere in the Powder River country of northern Wyoming and eastern Montana, three columns of troops were to take the field in a great pincer movement. Moving westward from Fort Abraham Lincoln, located south of present Mandan, North Dakota, a column, known as the Dakota Column, was to march toward the confluence of the Powder and Yellowstone rivers. From Fort Fetterman, located at the mouth of LaPrele Creek, near Douglas, Wyoming, another column under the command of Brigadier General George Crook was to move northward toward the Yellowstone, while Colonel John Gibbon was to lead a force consisting of components of the Seventh Infantry and the Second Cavalry eastward from the Montana forts. It was hoped that somewhere in the wild country between the Little Missouri and the Big Horn rivers the hostile bands of Sioux and Northern Cheyennes would be rounded up and either destroyed or forced to return to their agencies.

General Crook's column was the first to get under way and the first to strike the Indians. Moving north in the dead of winter in deep snows and such intense cold that the mercury often congealed in the bulb, a detachment of cavalry under the command of Colonel J. J. Reynolds, on the morning of March 17, struck and destroyed a mixed Sioux and Cheyenne village on the upper Powder River. Although the attack was a complete surprise and the troops succeeded in gaining complete possession of the village, Colonel Reynolds not only failed to follow up his victory but instead ordered a withdrawal. This enabled the Indians to seize the initiative, and after a series of misfortunes, the column returned to Fort Fetterman with little besides a crop of courts-martial to show for its sacrifices. On May 29, Crook again moved northward and on June 16 encountered a force of Sioux and Cheyennes on upper Rosebud Creek, where, after a day-long battle, he was stopped in his tracks. The column now retired to a base camp on Goose Creek, near present Sheridan, Wyoming, from which its commander dispatched a hurried call for reinforcements.

Because of a sudden eruption of partisan politics in which General Custer incurred the hostility of President Grant, the Dakota Column did not move westward until the seventeenth of May, and then with Custer in command only of his regiment, the Seventh United States Cavalry, the over-all command of the expedition which Custer had expected would be his having been given to the Department commander, Brigadier General Alfred H. Terry, who had taken over the responsibility at the specific request of General Sheridan. After a march that was almost without incident the column arrived at a point on the Powder River about twenty miles from its mouth in the late afternoon of June 7. From here Major Marcus A. Reno, with the six troops comprising the right wing of the regiment, was sent on a scouting tour up to the forks of the Powder and then across to Tongue River. The remainder of the Terry command moved to the mouth of Powder River, where a temporary base camp was established. Here the infantry companies and the wagon train were left, and the six companies of the left wing of the Seventh marched to the appointed rendezvous at the mouth of Tongue River.

On March 17, 1876, the same day that Crook was fighting the Indians on the upper Powder River, five companies of the Seventh Infantry marched from Fort Shaw. Their immediate destination was Fort Ellis, where they were joined by four troops, or companies, of the Second Cavalry, and put in motion across Bozeman Pass to the Yellowstone River, so that all told the Montana Column was composed of six companies of infantry and four of cavalry. The original intention had been to cross the Yellowstone River and march eastward over the Bozeman Trail toward old Fort C. F. Smith, but the news of Crook's fiasco on the Powder caused a change in plan, and instead, the column moved down the valley of the Yellowstone River, occasionally being forced to ford that stream, but for the most part keeping to the north bank. After reaching a point almost opposite the mouth of Tongue River, communications with the Dakota column were established and plans concerted for common action against an Indian village believed to be located at or near the confluence of the Big Horn and Little Big Horn rivers.

Although Major Reno had been expected to descend the Tongue River to its confluence with the Yellowstone, he did not do so, but went farther west and came out at the mouth of Rosebud Creek. He brought news of the Indians that the command had been seeking, however, for on the Rosebud his command had discovered a great Indian trail made by thousands of trailing lodge-poles. Custer, with his entire regiment, was to move up Rosebud Creek and follow the Indian trail. The Montana Column, which General Terry accompanied, was to move up the north bank of the Yellowstone until opposite the mouth of the Big Horn, where it would be ferried across that stream by the river steamer *Far West* and then move up the Big Horn and Tullock's Creek and across a plateau or tableland to the Little Big Horn, where it was believed the hostile Indian village would be found. Thus the Indians would be caught between the two commands. Since Gibbon, whose command included infantry, could not reach any point on the Little Big Horn until at least the morning of the twenty-sixth, Custer was instructed not to push his march too rapidly but to give Gibbon adequate time to get into position.

The Seventh Cavalry marched from the mouth of Rosebud Creek at noon on the twenty-second. Gibbon's command was already underway, and on the twenty-fourth was put across to the south bank of the Yellowstone and started up the Big Horn to a rendezvous with the shattered remnant of a once-proud regiment, which as a result of the disaster has become probably the best known in American military annals. On the night of the twenty-fourth, while Gibbon's command camped on Tullock's Creek, the Seventh Cavalry bivouacked on or near the present site of Busby, Montana. After a night march made for the purpose of getting as close to the enemy as possible with the intention of attacking early on the morning of the twenty-sixth, Custer came to the probably correct conclusion that the presence of his command had been discovered by the hostiles, and fearful that the village would begin to break up and scatter, he decided on something almost unprecedented in Indian warfare, an attack in the middle of the day. Thereupon he led his command down into the valley of the Little Big Horn, into regimental immortality, and into a secure, if somewhat controversial, place in American history.

Lieutenant Bradley began his Journal with the departure of the five companies from Fort Shaw on the morning of March 17, and from then on he presents a day-by-day record of what transpired, so that from the very beginning we have a detailed picture of the progress of the expedition, of the hardships and the tribulations, of the frustrations and the occasional triumphs. The vicissitudes of the weather, ranging from deep snow and sub-zero temperatures of a Montana winter to the blistering, searing heat of midsummer, with hailstones and cloudbursts, are all faithfully recorded. But the recital is by no means one of unrelieved hardship, there were times when the column seemed to be enjoying a picnic rather than engaged in a punitive campaign against a savage and ruthless foe. Some gaiety was added by the Crow scouts, whose antics were a perpetual source of amusement as well as of irritation, since almost everything they did had the flavor of comic opera. Of them it can well be said that they at least kept the daily routine from becoming monotonous. But whether it was feast or famine, rain, sunshine, or snow, it was all part of the day's work, all part of the fact that, as a trooper of another command once expressed it, "soldiers were paid for being shot at." But it is one of the ironies of the campaign that the members of the Montana Column were to have very little experience in "being shot at." There was very little glory in fighting Indians, a fact that Lieutenant Bradley readily conceded, and what little there was, consisted, in the cynical words of Colonel Gibbon, of being shot by an Indian from behind a rock and having one's name spelled wrong in the newspapers.

But the Journal is much more than an account of a military command moving through unsettled country against a primitive foe. It reveals Lieutenant Bradley as a man of many talents, one with definite scientific and historical interests, a man of infinite curiosity, who was interested in almost every item that came under his observation. As the troops marched through the area that is today the state of Montana, he not only recorded their daily progress but also added what he called "historical notices of the country traversed." And upon occasion, as with the ruins of the fort reputedly built by Lewis and Clark, he did not hesitate to correct a local legend which he knew to be inaccurate. Later on, he included a short account of the gold discoveries that led to the first influx of settlers into Montana and to its creation as a territory by act of Congress in 1864. This rush of miners and prospectors into the region and their characteristic disregard of the rights of the natives caused the Indians to become somewhat restless, and this in turn led to the construction of a number of forts, such as Fort Shaw, Camp Baker, Fort Ellis, and Fort Benton, and their occupation by federal troops. In short, in the course of his narrative, Lieutenant Bradley gives an excellent summary of the principal events in the history of Montana down to the time of which he wrote.

Incidents in that history which are of more than casual interest are the accounts of Baker's Battle of 1872, in which the military escort of the party surveying the route of the Northern Pacific Railroad through the Yellowstone Valley was attacked by a large body of Sioux; and the details of the founding of Fort Pease on the Yellowstone River some seven miles below its confluence with the Big Horn. There is also an interesting account of the massacre by the Blackfoot Indians of the Immel-Jones party of fur traders (Bradley spells it "Emmill"), which may have taken place on the Yellowstone near where the Lieutenant says it did, although there is some evidence to indicate that it may have occurred farther downstream on the outskirts of the present city of Billings, and still other localities have been pointed out as the place where it occurred. It would be too much to expect Lieutenant Bradley to present a wholly accurate account of everything about which he wrote, and there are places where his narrative needs correction. Such is the case with his excellent discussion of the origin of the Crow tribe of Indians, a large part of which has been called into question by the advances of modern scholarship and which needs to be supplemented by George E. Hyde's *Indians of the High Plains* (Norman, University of Oklahoma Press, 1959). Nor is it beyond doubt that the garrison at Fort Pease was as happy to see Major

Brisbin's relief column as the army represented them as being.

Even after making due allowance for the fact that he had abundant opportunity to revise and alter his judgments, Lieutenant Bradley's commentaries on both men and events are of great value to anyone interested in our Indian wars. Moreover, it seems probable, judging from information available from other sources, that no significant alterations were made in the rewriting of the account. There was the usual amount of friction and jealousy among the officers of both the Seventh Infantry and the Second Cavalry—although it did not exist to the extent that it did among the officers of the Seventh Cavalry, where it possibly was a factor contributing to the disaster that overtook that regiment. While there is very little indication of the existence of this feeling in the pages of the Journal, it does show through occasionally. And it might be noted that Lieutenant Bradley did not refrain from direct criticism of his commanding officer. Of exceptional interest is Lieutenant Bradley's estimate of Custer's character and his understanding of Custer's orders. The Lieutenant's remarks on the Seventh Cavalry as it appeared on the bluffs across the Yellowstone furnish a good contemporary estimate of that regiment on the eve of disaster.

Possibly the greatest attribute of the Journal is the fact that its author was a gifted writer and that many of his descriptions fall into the category of pure literature. It would be difficult to equal his description of snow blindness. He also goes farther and suggests a means of prevention and mentions a cure, although it might be questioned whether in this case the remedy was not almost as bad as the affliction. Nor, for suspense, is it easy to equal his reports of two scouting expeditions into the hostile country south of the Yellowstone River. On the first occasion the scouting party discovered a great Indian village, with the smoke of many campfires blanketing the valley of the Tongue River; and on the other, the camp of the same bands of Indians on the lower Rosebud. The fact that the hostiles had moved nearer to the soldiers rather than away from them was mute evidence of their lack of fear of Gibbon's command. One need not be possessed of more than an average amount of military knowledge to appreciate the attitude of the Crow scouts, who displayed a much more detailed knowledge of the country, as well as more alacrity and enthusiasm, in moving out of the danger zone than they had displayed in moving in. It was not that the Crows were cowards, for they were not; it was simply that they were supreme realists and knew full well the price of detection by the Sioux. Nor can anyone with active military experience fail to appreciate Bradley's description of the ride of the scouting detachment toward a grove of cottonwoods which they well knew contained numbers of hostile Indians far in excess of their own small group. But good soldiers all, they rode forward without flinching. And Lieutenant Bradley's description of the grief of the Crow scouts at hearing the first news of the disaster of the Little Big Horn is a classic in the literature of the American West.

The Journal proper, as previously noted, comes to an abrupt end, with the Montana Column in camp on the site of the present Crow Agency. During the day not only had they received word directly from three of the Crow scouts that Custer's command had met with disaster, but there had been a number of occurrences which indicated that the Crows were speaking the truth. Many of the members of Colonel Gibbon's command were not only apprehensive about what had happened to Custer and his regiment but also filled with anxiety and foreboding about what might be in store for the Montana Column on the morrow. But so tenacious is the will to believe, or as in this case, the will not to believe, that, as

Lieutenant Bradley noted, there were officers who persisted in expressing the belief that Custer had been victorious and had destroyed the Indian village, and who could ingeniously explain away all appearances to the contrary. That these were destined to a rude awakening on the morning of the twenty-seventh goes without saying.

The Journal ends at this point, but the next day Bradley's detachment was scouting ahead and to the left of the main column when it came on the bodies of the men and horses of Custer's five companies. Shortly afterwards they established communication with the beleaguered command of Major Reno and Captain Benteen. After rescuing the survivors, they gave the dead at least the semblance of a burial, and the wounded were transported on mule litters to the mouth of the Little Big Horn, where the river steamer *Far West* was waiting. Then the combined commands marched overland to the junction of the Big Horn River with the Yellowstone. From here the news of the disaster was sent out to a shocked and unbelieving nation while the soldiers settled down to a period of inactivity until further orders—and reinforcements—could arrive. On the ninth of July, Lieutenant Bradley left for Fort Ellis, thus accounting for his presence in Helena on the twenty-fifth. But for everyone concerned the remainder of the campaign was anticlimax, the triumph of the red man that sultry day on the dust-covered ridge above the Little Big Horn was to prove to be transitory and illusive, and the details of his final subjugation were to be neither romantic nor heroic.

The "Journal of James H. Bradley: The Sioux Campaign of 1876 under the Command of General John Gibbon, preceded by a Brief Biography of Lieutenant Bradley" was first published in *Contributions to the Historical Society of Montana*, volume II (Helena, State Publishing Company, 1896).

It is reproduced here from that source. Lieutenant Bradley's letter to the editor of the Helena *Herald* is also in the files of the Society. My warmest thanks are returned to that society and its director, Michael Kennedy, for supplying the copy.

EDGAR I. STEWART

Eastern Washington College
Cheney, Washington
January 10, 1961

The March of the Montana Column

A Brief Biography of Lieutenant Bradley

LIEUTENANT JAMES H. BRADLEY was born in Sandusky County, Ohio, on the twenty-fifth of May, 1844. In April, 1861, at the early age of seventeen years, he enlisted as a private in the 14th Ohio Volunteers, as a member of which regiment he took part in the actions at Philippi, Laurel Hill, and Carrick's Ford, Virginia. After completing his term of service in the 14th he re-enlisted, this time entering the 45th Ohio Volunteers in June, 1862, and was discharged as a sergeant in July, 1865. During this period he was in action at Somers's, Monticello, and West Farms, Kentucky, and Philadelphia, E. Tennessee. He was taken prisoner in October, 1863, and held until March, 1864, when he rejoined his regiment and was engaged in the battles of Kenesaw Mountain, Peach Tree Creek, Jonesboro, Franklin, and Nashville, and in the siege of Atlanta. He was appointed second lieutenant, 18th U. S.

Infantry, on the twenty-third of February, 1866, and first lieutenant the twenty-ninth day of July, 1866, and was transferred to the 7th U. S. Infantry November 28, 1871.

While in the 18th Infantry, he was engaged against hostile Indians at Crazy Woman's Fork, in Wyoming. After joining the 7th Infantry, he was stationed at Forts Benton and Shaw, Montana, performing the usual routine duties of a frontier post. He was with the command of General Gibbon in the expedition against the hostile Sioux in 1876, and commanded a mounted detachment of the 7th Infantry during the campaign against the Nez Percé Indians in 1877, losing his life on the ninth of August while gallantly leading his detachment in the charge of the command against the camp of Chief Joseph and his band at the Big Hole, Montana.[1] Lieutenant

[1] "The valiant band of regulars and volunteers who had been sent down the river under Lieutenant Bradley to strike the lower end of the camp, now turned and fought their way up through it; through the willow thickets; through the willow sloughs and bayous; through the windings of the river; killing an Indian and losing a man at every turn, and finally joined the command in the woods.

"But the gallant young leader of the band was not there. He had fallen early in the fight; in fact, the first white man killed. He was leading the left wing of the army in its assault on the camp. General Gibbon had cautioned him to exercise great care going into the brush at that point, and told him to keep under cover of the brush and river bank as much as possible, but the brave young man knew no fear and made his men follow him. One of them called to him just as he was entering a thicket where a party of Indians were believed to be lurking, and said: 'Hold on, Lieutenant; don't go in there; it's sure death.' But he pressed on, regardless of his own safety, and just as he reached the edge of the brush an Indian raised up within a few feet of him and fired, killing him instantly.

"The Indian was immediately riddled with bullets, and then the men charged madly into and through the brush, dealing death to every Indian who came in their way, and the blood of many a redskin crimsoned the sod, whose life counted against that of this gallant young officer. Thus he, who had led the night march over the mountains; who had by day, with his comrades, crawled up, located, and reconnoitered the Indian camp, and sent the news of his discovery to his chief; who had on the following night aided that chief so signally in moving his command to the field and in planning the attack; who had gallantly led one wing of the little army in that fierce charge

Bradley was married to Miss Mary Beech, the daughter of Doctor Beech, of Atlanta, Georgia, and at his death left two daughters. His widow yet resides in Atlanta.

It may be truthfully said of Lieutenant Bradley as a soldier that he was a man absolutely without fear, and no murmur or objection escaped him against instructions or orders. Battle roused the spirit within him, and his young life was largely spent in its strife. His quiet demeanor did not shadow forth the dauntless courage that possessed him, but which his comrades discovered was his commanding and characteristic possession. In form he was not large, but lithe and supple, and seemed to have a constitution of iron; he was nervous and active, of keen observation, and perfectly tireless and enthusiastic in the work given him to do. He was no idler. If there was no routine duty in post or camp, his resources for activity never failed him. His comrades in peace and war loved and learned to respect him, his subordinates trusted to his judgment implicitly, and his superiors relied upon him with no distrust. They knew he had been taught in the school of General Thomas, the silent, cheerful, obstinate "rock of Chicamauga." They knew his patriotism, his courage, his resolve, his ambition, and that in forlorn hopes he had the audacity of

"Clan Ronald the dauntless and Moray the proud."

Lieutenant Bradley was one of the subordinate officers of the Army best known to the citizens of Montana. He was ever alert, and his commanding officers kept him moving on military errands wherever the occasion required. His researches into the early history of what is now Montana was with him

through the jungle and into the hostile camp, had laid down his noble life, and his comrades mourned him as a model officer, a good friend, a brave soldier."
[From *The Battle of the Big Hole*.]

a labor of love, and the diary published herewith is but a small part of the manuscripts which he left at his decease. Through the intelligent interest of General Gibbon, who was his commanding officer here, seconded by the efforts of Lieutenant Bradley's wife, these papers came into the possession of the Historical Society. In the shadows of the Rocky Mountains, Lieutenant Bradley gave his life for his country. As in Montana, and to defend her pioneers, he died dutifully, it seems fitting that the Historical Society should perpetuate his fame; and yet other papers from his prolific pen may be expected in future volumes of our contributions.[2]

[2] The identity of the author of this "brief biography" published with the Journal in *Contributions to the Montana Historical Society*, II (1896), is not revealed. Nor are the writers of the footnotes identified other than by initials. It can be guessed that "H. S. W." is perhaps Harry S. Wheeler, then librarian of the Historical Society of the State of Montana, but could "W. E. S." be honorary member W. Egbert Smith? It can also be conjectured that most of the unsigned notes and those signed "J. H. B." are Bradley's own, though in a few instances it seems that they, also, must have been added. The present editor's notes are identified also by his initials, E. I. S. (Edgar I. Stewart). [Publisher's note.]

Journal of James H. Bradley

ABOUT TEN O'CLOCK A. M. the battalion formed on the parade ground and breaking in column of fours from the right to march to the left moved out of the post, and took the Helena road. The five companies, including the mounted detachment, number 12 officers and 195 men, and are accompanied by ten wagons containing camp equipage, extra ammunition, the personal effects of officers and men, and ten days' rations—which are expected to last until the command reaches Fort Ellis.

General Gibbon, for the present, remains behind with Lieutenants Jacobs and Burnett, intending to join us at some point in advance, the command of the column devolving in the

---

[1] Fort Shaw was located on the Sun River, not far from present Great Falls, Montana. Some of the buildings are still standing.—E. I. S.

mean time upon Captain Rawn. The captains are all mounted, the lieutenants, except Woodruff, battalion adjutant and commanding the Gatling gun, and myself, commanding the mounted detachment, being on foot. The country is all under snow to the depth of several inches. Weather calm but quite cold in the morning, turning very cold in the afternoon when a keen and piercing wind sprung up that drifted the snow about and filled the air with the flying particles. After a march of eleven miles the command camped at 3:30 P. M. at Eagle Rock.

Keating and McFarland of Co. K deserted last night, and I received orders to attempt their capture with the mounted detachment. Finding their trail, which led toward Helena, I followed the tracks with eight men, leaving the post at the same time that the command marched. We reached Krueger's ranch, forty-one miles from Fort Shaw, at half-past eight in the evening, took supper, fed the horses, and rested until 11 P. M., and then pushed on with three men, leaving the rest to join the command. Traveled all night, with the mercury showing thirty degrees below zero and snow filling the air, and reached Johns's ranch about 5 A. M.—distance sixty-three miles.

Saturday, 18. Passed two hours at Johns's, breakfasting, feeding the horses, resting, and making inquiries after my deserters. As nothing could be learned of them, I concluded that they had turned off some distance back onto the Mullan road.[2] At 7 A. M. we took saddle once more and crossed over to this road, there finding their tracks—which we recognized by the peculiar shoeing of their horses. As the track was fresh, we pressed on rapidly, and caught a distant view of them as

2 Named for Lieutenant John Mullan, this road connected Fort Walla Walla, on the Columbia River, with Fort Benton, the head of river navigation on the Missouri River.—E. I. S.

8

we neared Helena, reaching Widow Durgin's house, four miles out of the town, only fifteen minutes behind them.

Here they had paused and left their compliments for certain officers of the regiment, and then ridden off on the Corinne road.[3] Followed at a gallop and overtook them four miles beyond Helena at 1 P.M., having traveled about eighty-four miles since ten o'clock yesterday morning. They surrendered without resistance, and were soon lodged in the Helena jail. Quartered my men at the Overland Hotel, and I registered at the St. Louis.

The command broke camp at Eagle Rock at 8 A.M. and marched to Dearborn River, seventeen miles, camping on that stream at 4 P.M., the wagons arriving at the camp an hour later. There were several inches of loose snow on the road, greatly impeding the march and wearying the men.

It was a bright day, and the dazzling glare from the snow seriously affected the men's eyes. The night was intensely cold, and all suffered much. There was no thermometer at hand, but experienced judges pronounced it at least forty degrees below zero. The lieutenants discovered this morning that there were a number of extra horses with the column, and notwithstanding they had been occupied for a month previous in breaking in shoes and training their legs for the campaign by daily excursions of from three to five miles, the discovery of these horses diffused among them universal joy. With eager alacrity they volunteered their services to ride, and it was noticed from this day forth that up hill or down, muddy or dry, cold or warm, none stuck to their saddles with more invincible determination, more unflagging constancy and zeal than the "subs" thus fortuitously provided with a mount. There were nearly enough of these extra horses to go

[3] Corinne Road connected the infant Montana settlements with the Union Pacific Railroad at Corinne, Utah.—E. I. S.

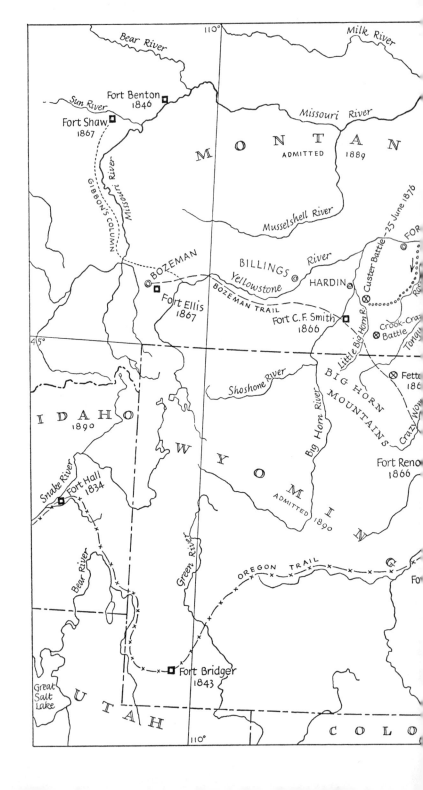

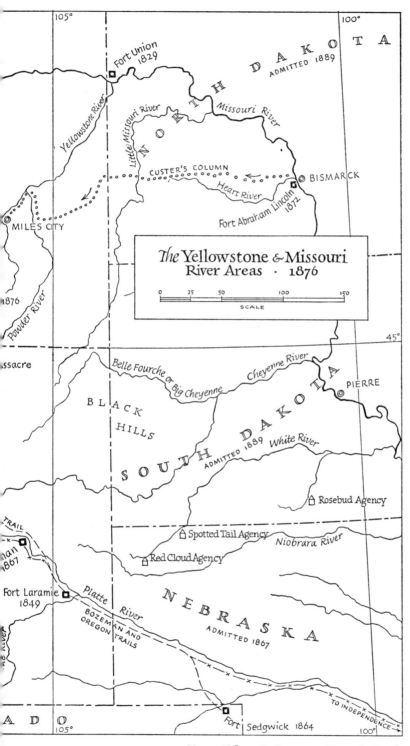

The Yellowstone & Missouri River Areas · 1876

0   25   50   100   150
SCALE

From Edgar I. Stewart, *Custer's Luck*

around, and by changing about, all had frequent opportunities to ride. Only Lieutenant Coolidge disdained such aid,
whose excellent pedestrian abilities won for him the regula-
tion of the marches and halts, and henceforth throughout the
campaign, with a sturdy sergeant at his side, he was to be
seen leading the column at a twenty-eight-inch step as nearly
one hundred and ten to the minute as frequent reference to
a watch could secure.

Sunday, 19. The command marched at 8 A. M. and made a
severe and toilsome march through deep snow drifts to Kreuger's ranch, thirteen miles, reaching their camping ground in
Kreuger's garden at 1 P. M. Throughout the forenoon there
was a succession of sunshine and shadow, with the snow flying
in clouds and a bitterly cold air. Captain Rawn became
seriously snowblind and was compelled to resign the command to Captain Freeman, next in rank. Many of the men
suffered from the same cause, and there were also several
cases of freezing of more or less severity. Lieutenant Kendrick and Dr. Hart were among the unfortunate victims of
the frost, whose icy fingers, judging by the singular experience
of these gentlemen, were unrestrained by any considerations
of delicacy. Many of the company commanders had provided their men with blue or green veils as a protection
against snow-blindness, but these proved wholly inadequate.
In fact they were rather an aggravation of the difficulty, as
they impeded the sight and annoyed the eyes with their constant flapping to and fro in the wind. After reaching camp,
the command was compelled to wait two hours for the arrival
of its wagons. Some of these were overturned in the course
of the day's march, and what with such accidents, the hilly
character of the country, and the bad roads, did not come
up until 3 o'clock.

I had designed to rejoin the command today with my prisoners, but found on getting up and going into the light that I was a victim of snow-blindness. I had gone to the jail to give orders about my prisoners, when I discovered my sight failing and was scarcely able to reach the hotel ere I became totally blind. The loss of sight comes on with a feeling such as is created by smoke in the eyes, that, if the case is a severe one, soon increases into the most intense burning pain. The eyes cannot bear the light and the eyeballs seem to roll in liquid fire with a grating feeling as though in contact with particles of sand. The temptation to bandage them or apply water is great, but should be resisted, as the one heats the eyes and the other increases the irritation, and the pain is only intensified. This blindness seems principally confined to high latitudes, but I have heard of occasional cases as far south as the plains of western Kansas. It is mainly brought on by the exposure of the eyes to the glare of the sun upon the snow, but is accelerated and aggravated by high wind and flying snow; and it is most likely to occur late in the winter season and early in the spring when the sun's rays fall with a more vertical slant. Indeed, in early and mid-winter, cases of snow-blindness are extremely rare. The Indians and even wild animals are subject to it, and to the frequenter of our western plains a snow-blind rabbit or even sage or prairie chicken is no uncommon sight. A method of treatment practiced by some of the northwestern Indians is to drop into the corner of the eye a little skunk oil, which they extract and preserve for this purpose. I have been assured by old hunters who have tried it that it is a sovereign remedy. But prevention is infinitely preferable to cure, and may be affected by blackening the face to the distance of an inch or more around the eyes close up to the lids. This has never failed me, and I have yet to hear of an instance where it did not secure immunity from this terrible malady. A bit of wet powder or lampblack, the soot off the bottom of a kettle, a charred stick, or powdered charcoal will accomplish this. It is the approved method of warding it off practiced by frontiersmen. In the month of May, 1867, in the days of my inexperience on the "Plains," I had thirty men out of a command of forty disabled in this manner as the result of one day's march through the snow on a sunny day, myself being the greatest sufferer, as my duties compelled me to use my eyes most. The number of the well was barely sufficient to attend to the afflicted, and we lay several days almost defenseless in an Indian country. I have enlarged upon this subject somewhat as the information will be new to many of the readers, while the hints I have given may save some inexperienced young officer, or other person, from acquiring his knowledge of it at such bitter cost as I have acquired mine.

My case in this instance proved a severe one, and I took to my room and sent for a physician, leaving my prisoners in jail and ordering my three men to rejoin the command. For several days I was *hors du combat*, suffering tortures like to those of the damned; but Montana's most eminent physician, Dr. J. S. Glick, after examining me and announcing that I was good for thirty days of it, astonished himself by curing me completely in five.

Monday, 20. Captain Rawn found himself this morning, from the condition of his eyes, wholly incapacitated for command, and returned to Fort Shaw, proper treatment being impossible on the march. His case proved to be a stubborn one, and it was several weeks before he was sufficiently recovered to attempt to rejoin the command. At Fort Ellis, while en route to the command, he suffered a relapse, and was once more forced to return.

The command marched at 7:15 A.M., advanced eighteen miles, and camped at 2:15 P.M. in a picturesque cove in the

Little Prickly Pear Cañon. The weather had moderated, the snow melted rapidly, and the men splashed on through slush and mud all day, and pitched their tents in mud at night. Yesterday—intense cold, the men freezing; today—a summer temperature and a waste of water and mud. Such are the changes in this climate. Surely the command has had an unpleasant enough beginning. Though their couch was soft enough in all conscience, wet blankets and clothes did not conduce to pleasant dreams upon the part of our patient two hundred that night.

Tuesday, 21. It was discovered this morning that two men had deserted during the night. One of them, considered rather a simple-minded fellow, had been cunning enough to walk backward through the snow for a mile or so, but was caught for all that. The other man got safely off. The command marched at 7 A.M., but after proceeding only five miles went into camp at 9:30 A.M., near Johns's ranch,[4] to enable the men to dry their clothes and bedding, the day being pleasant and warm. Lieutenant Burnett came up today on the coach but passed on to Helena.

Wednesday, 22. Command marched at 7 A.M. The road was dry and hard and the men were troubled with blistered feet. After a march of seventeen miles camp was pitched at 1:30 P.M., near the dwelling of widow Durgin, about four miles from Helena. General Gibbon and Lieutenant Jacobs came up in a buggy and passed on to Helena. A number of the officers and some of the men were permitted to visit the city in the afternoon and evening. The two deserters I had arrested were taken from the jail to the camp and released and restored to duty without trial. Dr. Hart remained in the

[4] Johns' ranch is situated near the head of Little Prickly Pear Cañon, on the old Helena and Fort Benton stage road, and between Silver and Mitchell stations on the Montana Central R'y.—H. S. W.

city sick, and did not again join the command. In the absence of a medical officer, Lieutenant Coolidge was appointed acting surgeon. He had amused himself for some years past by employing his leisure in the study of medicine, and is well qualified for the post.

Thursday, 23. The command marched at 6:45 A. M., one man less by desertion last night. The road was exceedingly muddy, and it proved a hard day on the men. As Lieutenant Woodruff phrased it, "The march was only eighteen miles long to-day but six inches deep all the way"; and the men camped near the "Spokane House," a wayside inn, at 2 P. M., thoroughly tired out.

Friday, 24. The command broke camp at 6:30 A. M. and marched over a fair road seventeen miles, camping at 1:30 P. M. on the Missouri River, at Indian Creek ferry. I rejoined the command at this camp, by stage from Helena, Dr. Glick having pronounced me fit for duty again. Resumed command of the mounted detachment, which in my absence had been in Lieutenant Woodruff's charge. Sick call, according to a fashion that the boys have fallen into, was received with cheers and groans all over the camp, that deterred many a poor devil who needed treatment for sore limbs and feet from presenting himself at the doctor's tent. But the march had told upon the men, unaccustomed to it as they were, and there was a pretty respectable attendance at the hospital of men too badly off to care for ridicule. The worst cases are allowed to ride on the wagons. But the men are toughening to their work, and will be all right in a few days. I notice that Dr. *alias* Lieutenant Coolidge examined his patients and prescribed his remedies with the unction of a professional.

Saturday, 25. Broke camp at 6:30 A. M., and camped near Galen's residence at 2:45 P. M., after a march of twenty-one miles. Lieutenant Coolidge, who marched on foot, says in his journal "weather warm"; while I, who rode, chronicled in mine "cold wind all day." Road mainly good, but the last few miles quite muddy. Camped in the mud—the best we could do.

Sunday, 26. Marched at 6:15 A.M., and as the Madison bridge was down, turned to the left and crossed the Missouri River at the ferry something less than a mile below the junction of the Jefferson and Madison and a couple of hundred yards above the mouth of the Gallatin.

The question arose among the officers as to where the Missouri properly begins: at the junction of the Jefferson and Madison, or a mile lower down where the Gallatin joins its waters to those of the other two streams. Upon inquiry, it was found that local usage—which ought to govern—favors the former. As I interpret Lewis and Clark (who conferred these names), they intended it so.

Soon after crossing the ferry we passed the few straggling houses known as Gallatin City, and camped on the plain half a mile beyond at 12:45 P.M., having marched fourteen miles. General Gibbon and Lieutenant Jacobs came up soon after we formed camp, returning to the hotel for lodgings after spending some time with us.

Within sight of our camp the "mighty Missouri" takes its rise and begins its eventual journey of 3,000 and some hundred miles to the Mississippi. Both from this circumstance and from the history connected with it, the locality is one of the most interesting in Montana, it being here that the first fur-trading establishment on the upper Missouri stood, and not far distant, on the Jefferson River, that occurred the wonderful escape of John Colter, a discharged member of Lewis and Clark's command—the narrative of which has thrilled the hearts of thousands of readers. I was aware of the existence of this old fort and knew something of its history, and was therefore induced to pass the afternoon making personal search and diligent inquiry after any possible remaining traces of it that would indicate the spot where it had stood. Toward night I found what I sought, but too late to make personal examination of the little that remains. The good people of that neighborhood call it "Lewis and Clark's Fort," and relate to the interested inquirer how these famous captains passed a winter in it on their way across the continent, concealing in a *cache* near by a large amount of valuable property. This fabled *cache* has given rise to an investigating spirit almost equal to that once displayed in the search for the buried treasure of Captain Kidd, and a deal of useless digging has been done in the neighborhood. I have found this error concerning the fort prevalent even among intelligent, well-informed men, and am therefore induced to make it the occasion of the first of these "historical notices of the country traversed."

The Missouri Fur Company[5]

The accounts brought back by Lewis and Clark, in 1806, of the fur-bearing resources of the country drained by the Missouri River and its upper tributaries excited great interest among the fur-trading inhabitants of the then little frontier town of St. Louis. One of the most enterprising, Mr. Manuel Lisa, who had previously traded up the lower Missouri, in the spring of 1807 led a trading party up the Missouri and Yellowstone rivers to the mouth of the Big Horn, where he built a fort—the first civilized establishment in Montana or upon the upper Missouri and its tributary streams. He re-

[5] Lieut. Bradley, in his list of references relative to the Missouri Fur Co., refers to Washington Irving's *Astoria*. His account of this company is evidently largely taken from that work. His other references are: *St. Louis Democrat, Appleton's Journal, Lippincott's Gazetteer,* and Major Culbertson.— H. S. W.

mained nine months, trading principally with the Crow Indians, and in 1808 broke up the establishment and returned to St. Louis, having made a remunerative trade. His favorable representations, added to the information communicated by Lewis and Clark, induced a number of St. Louis merchants to unite with him in the formation of an association which took the name of the Missouri Fur Company. There were twelve partners, with a united capital of forty thousand dollars, a sum by no means adequate to the vast plans of the company, though larger than that with which the famous Hudson's Bay Company began its existence which spread its posts over half the continent.

It was the design of the company to abandon the timid methods of the former trade, plunge at once deep into the wilderness, ascend the stream to its uttermost navigable waters, and by establishing posts at the most available points monopolize the trade of the entire region. It had in its employ about 250 men—partly American hunters, but mainly Creoles and Canadian voyageurs, who in various flotillas, conducted by some of the partners, were put in motion, and before the close of the year 1809 posts had been established among the Sioux, Arickarees, and Mandans, and a principal one, whose garrison comprised the larger part of the company's employees, "at the Three Forks of the Missouri."

This post was in the heart of the country then possessed by the Piegan tribe of the Blackfeet Indians, whose hostility it was hoped might be appeased, both for the sake of their trade and because the hundreds of small streams which rise in the adjacent mountains and unite to form the Missouri abounded with beaver, which the company's servants were to be employed in trapping. But the Blackfeet were in communication with the posts of the British traders upon the Saskatchewan, from which they obtained arms, ammunition, and all the commodities of civilization required in their wild life, so that they were wholly independent of this fort. Besides, in consequence of the killing of one of their number by Captain Lewis in 1806, they had conceived the most violent hatred of the Americans, a feeling carefully fostered by the British traders to prevent competition, and they had fiercely declared that they would rather hang the scalp of an American to their girdle than kill a buffalo to keep from starving. Animated by such implacable and vindictive resentment, they not only failed to become the customers of the fort, but set themselves at work to effect the destruction of its garrison. They lurked incessantly in the vicinity of the post, sought to ambuscade the hunters, attacked every party over whom they could gain any advantage, and almost entirely frustrated the trapping system that had been inaugurated. It became dangerous to go any distance from the fort except in large parties, and in one case a party of twenty men were assailed by surprise and nine killed. Not less than twenty of the garrison lost their lives in the various conflicts that took place, and it was estimated that double that number of Indians were killed.

It had been expected that three hundred packs of beaver would be secured the first year, and but for the hostility of the Blackfeet, the expectation would probably have been realized. As it was, there were scarcely twenty packs. With this meager return the greater portion of the party descended the river the next spring (1809), while the remainder continued to be cooped up in the fort not daring to hunt and suffering for want of provisions. At last, finding the situation so irksome and unprofitable and fearing the destruction of his little band, Mr. Henry, the partner who had been left in charge, determined in the fall to move over into the country of the more pacific Shoshonnees and winter upon one of the head branches of the Columbia. Crossing the mountains with great difficulty and suffering—for winter overtook them and game was scarce —he found a pleasant location, where timber was plentiful, upon the North or Henry's Fork of Snake River, where he established himself and built a new fort—the first American establishment (except the wintering house of Lewis and Clark) west of the Rocky Mountains.

Meanwhile no tidings of him were received at St. Louis, and the company, ignorant of his movements, were apprehensive that he had been massacred. At length, no longer able to control their anxiety, early in 1811 an expedition was set on foot to go in quest of him. It started about the beginning of February, under the command of Mr. Lisa, in a swift barge propelled by twenty oars and armed with a swivel mounted at the bow, the whole number of persons on board being twenty-six. In the meantime his isolation and the poverty of his Snake customers induced Mr. Henry to recross the mountains and return to the East. Arriving at the Missouri, he built boats, upon which his party embarked; and thus it happened that Lisa, sweeping in his light barge easily and pleasantly up stream, and Henry with his little fleet dropping down with the current, met each other at the Arickaree village, in the neighborhood of the present city of Bismarck, about the middle of June.

Mr. Henry's stay beyond the mountains had not been unprofitable, and he took down with him forty packs of beaver —a far better return than could reasonably have been anticipated. To render this account of the operations of the company complete, I will add that the hostility of the Blackfeet and the consequent ruin of their prospects in this quarter were not the only misfortune that had been sustained by the company. The establishments among the Mandans and Arickarees had proved unprofitable, and besides the Sioux factory was accidentally burned, occasioning an estimated loss of fifteen thousand dollars—almost half the original capital of the company. The term of the association expired in 1811, but notwithstanding the unforseen difficulties and disasters that had beset its first efforts, it was found on balancing accounts that the company had its capital of forty thousand dollars yet intact, and, in addition, the three establishments below the Yellowstone. A reorganization was effected, and though no further attempt was made to trade in the Blackfeet country the business of the company elsewhere was extensive and the profits large. It enjoyed a deserved prosperity until the business prostration occasioned by the War of 1812, when it was forced to suspend operations and finally dissolved.

The fort built by this company "at the Three Forks of the Missouri" is the establishment whose traces still remain near Gallatin City and which is popularly ascribed to Lewis and Clark. In 1870, the outlines of the fort were still intact, from which it appears that it was a double stockade of logs set three feet deep, enclosing an area of about three hundred feet square, situated upon the tongue of land (at that point half a mile wide) between the Jefferson and Madison rivers, about two miles above their confluence, upon the south bank of a channel of the former stream now called Jefferson Slough. Since then the stream has made such inroads upon the land that only a small portion of the fort—the southwest angle—remains. It is probable that every vestige of this old relic will soon disappear, except the few stumps of stockade logs that have been removed by two or three gentlemen of antiquarian tastes. When Henry abandoned the fort, a blacksmith's anvil was left behind, which remained there for thirty or forty years undisturbed, gazed upon only by the Indians, who regarded it with supersitition and awe. At last it disappeared and it is said to have been found and removed by a party of white men. Can any reader of this volume give an account of its fate? It ought to be among the relics of the Montana Historical Society.

Monday, 27. Marched at 6:10 A. M., and camped near Cockerill's bridge over the West Gallatin at 12:45 P. M., eighteen miles. The men are now well broken in and marched like veterans, blistered feet and stiffened limbs being a rarity. Lost two men by desertion last night—the last to leave us in this manner. This makes nine in all, only three of the number having been apprehended. The General and Lieutenant Jacobs passed on to Fort Ellis.

Tuesday, 28. Broke camp at 6:15 A. M., just after sunrise. The men pushed on with the stride of old campaigners, and seemed to glory in their newly developed marching powers. Road quite muddy as we neared Bozeman. Marched through the town and passed on to Fort Ellis, nearly four miles beyond, camping near the post at 12 M., having advanced 16 miles. Again the men are under the necessity of making down their beds in the mud, as the whole country around Ellis is a wash of slush and mud, with torrents of dirty water sweeping down the slope on which our camp is pitched. We were very hospitably received by the garrison, the cavalry portion of which has but recently returned from a trip down the Yellowstone to succor the garrison of the trading post of Fort F. D. Pease.[6] They are now preparing to join us in the campaign. The interchange of civilities that followed, the invitations to dinners and breakfasts, the calls, the convivial reunions, the—but why particularize?—are they not written in the book of our memories?

[6] On this episode see Edgar I. Stewart, "Major Brisbin's Relief of Fort Pease," *Montana, the Magazine of Western History,* Vol. VI, No. 3, (July, 1956) 23–28.—E. I. S.

Wednesday, 29. We remained in camp today, drawing
rations and forage, and preparing generally for the second
heat in our campaign. At this point we are to cut loose from
the settlements, having in our front only a few isolated cabins,
whose owners occupy them in continual peril of their lives;
and before taking this plunge into the wilderness, it will conduce to the better understanding of the situation upon the
part of those of my readers who do not dwell within the Territory, and perhaps profit somewhat those who do, to take a
brief glance of the country we are to leave behind.

A Glance at Montana

Not to be too minute, it is sufficient here to say that in the
year 1860 there was nothing within the limits of what is now
Montana that could be termed a settlement, its few white
inhabitants being of that zealous and adventurous sort who
precede civilization as missionaries, hunters, trappers, traders,
and idlers in Indian camps. A Mr. John Owen had a trading
post in the Bitter Root valley, called after himself Fort Owen;
the American Fur Company—as the firm of Pierre Choteau,
Jr. & Co. was popularly called—maintained its old post of
Fort Benton on the Missouri River; there were two Catholic
missions located respectively among the Coeur d'Alene and
Flathead Indians. Beyond these there was nothing in all Montana to mark the presence of civilized man except the temporary shelters of the vagrant class who occupied them today
and tomorrow sought an abiding place elsewhere.

But, from the throngs that passed to and fro along the Cali-
fornia and Oregon trails, individuals and small parties in
course of time turned off into the wild and unknown regions
of the north, and ransacking among the sands of its thousand
streams ere long discovered that they were liberally sprinkled

with golden particles stolen by the predatory waters from nature's treasure-vaults in the rocky recesses of the hills. The first discovery is credited to François Finlay, in 1852, but he did not seek to profit by it and nothing came of it. In 1856 a mountaineer named Silverthorne appeared at Fort Benton with gold dust to the amount of $1,525.00, which he claimed to have mined in the mountains of this Territory and disposed of it in trade. It would seem that he afterwards went to California to form a party to return to his mines. James and Granville Stuart[7] and Rezin Anderson prospected some in 1857, but it was not till 1862 that the new-found gold fields attracted much attention and began to draw hither the crowds that have made Montana what it is. A town sprang up in the vicinity of the mines, called first La Barge City, but renamed Deer Lodge two years later, followed the same year by the rise of Bannack, where new and valuable discoveries had been made. Prospecting parties spread themselves over the country, and in 1863 by a lucky accident the vast treasures of Alder Gulch were brought to light, giving rise to the towns of Summit, Virginia, and Nevada, which turned out $30,000,000 in the first three years of their existence. So rapidly had population sought the new gold fields that in 1864 it is estimated that Alder Gulch alone contained 14,000 souls; and Congress deemed it advisable to create a new territory out of the country thus suddenly developed, by carving off a slice each from Dakota and Idaho and continuing them under the name of Montana, the Organic Act for this purpose receiving the approval of the President on the 26th day of May, 1864.

New discoveries continued to be occasionally made, and at last in the fall of 1864, a party of twenty-five men, led by Uncle John Cowan, began mining in the Last Chance Gulch

[7] Granville Stuart is now, 1895, U. S. minister to Uruguay and Paraguay; he was appointed by President Cleveland in 1894.

in diggings discovered the previous July. From this humble beginning arose the City of Helena, for the diggings proved unexpectedly rich, and within a year had attracted thither not less than 8,000 souls. Thus, through the discovery of the golden grains that for ages had rested unnoticed in her streams, this remote region, buried in the center of a continent, had, from a savage wilderness tenanted only by wild beasts and wilder men, become the seat of several populous towns and the home of 20,000 inhabitants, with most of the appliances of a civilized community and the trades, professions, and business incident thereto.

But the savage tribes which had hitherto maintained over this wide region undisputed sway were restless under the encroachments of the new-comers and finally broke into open hostility. Then, in the spring of 1866, the 13th infantry was ordered up the Missouri River to take post in the new Territory. Camp Cooke was established on the Missouri, 120 miles below Fort Benton, and in the following year Fort Shaw, on Sun River, and Fort Ellis, on East Gallatin, and, in 1869, Camp Baker on Smith's River, or Deep Creek, were added to the defenses of the Territory. In the latter year Camp Cooke was abandoned, what remained of the garrison being removed to Fort Benton. In December, 1869, four companies of the 2d cavalry were added to the garrison at Fort Ellis, where they have remained ever since; and in June, 1870, seven companies of the 7th infantry arrived in Montana, relieving the 13th, to which were added the other three companies in 1872. For some years the disposition of the troops in the Territory has been as follows: Headquarters and six companies, 7th infantry, at Fort Shaw; one company, 7th infantry, and four companies, 2nd cavalry, at Fort Ellis; two companies, 7th infantry, at Camp Baker; and one company, 7th infantry, at Fort Benton: the whole constituting the District of Montana, commanded the greater part of the time by Colonel John Gibbon, 7th infantry. Detachments of these commands have occasionally been stationed elsewhere as emergencies arose, but only temporarily.

The population of Montana at the present time is only about 15,000, but there are permanent residents—here to stay. They are engaged mainly in mining, agriculture, and stock raising, with such a proportion of other trades and industries as are needed by a community of this size; and are gathered generally in the vicinity of the towns, which are at considerable distance from each other and separated by wide stretches of country comparatively unoccupied. In some of the richer valleys for a space of several miles the farm houses succeed each other at small intervals up and down the stream, approximating somewhat in appearance to the farming communities of the East. In the towns—especially in Helena, the present Capital—many of the buildings are of a substantial and expensive character. The people are unusually intelligent, moral, industrious, and enterprising. The best illustration of this is the fact that they support ten newspapers, two of which publish daily editions, all thriving, well-conducted, and very readable. Such is the community we are about to leave behind us—a community in the heart of a desert with hundreds of miles of uninhabited wilderness stretching away on every side of it, dissevering it from the rest of the civilized world as completely as though it were on an island in mid-ocean.

Thursday, 30. Resumed the march this morning at 7:30 A. M., heading for the Yellowstone. The cavalry is not yet ready, but will follow in a few days. General Gibbon and staff remain behind but will come on with the cavalry. Our route led through the gap and over the divide traversed by Captain Clark in July, 1806, upon his return from the Pacific. This expedition it will be remembered, left St. Louis, or rather its vicinity, in May, 1804, ascended the Missouri to its source during that and the succeeding year, crossed the Rocky Mountains, and reached the Pacific Ocean in the fall of 1805. Here they passed the following winter, and began their return in the spring of 1806. Upon regaining the mountains, the party divided for the better exploration of the country, one detachment led by Captain Lewis crossing to the Marias River and proceeding down the Missouri; the other, by Captain Clark, which crossed to the upper waters of the Yellowstone, descending it and re-uniting with Captain Lewis upon the Missouri. It was upon the occasion of this separation that Captain Clark passed through the gap traversed by us today. The route is a difficult one, half piercing, half surmounting a high mountain range dividing the waters of the Missouri from those of the Yellowstone. Camped at noon upon Fleischman's Creek, a small stream rising in the gap and flowing into the Yellowstone; but it was two and a half hours later ere the wagons arrived. Marched ten and a half miles. The distances heretofore given conform to local usage, but those that will hereafter appear are derived from odometer measurements made during our march. Snow fell briskly in the afternoon. We learned today that General Crook, of the 17th infantry, attacked a large Sioux village on Little Powder River, drove away the Indians with considerable loss, captured and destroyed the camp, and also captured the greater part of the ponies but lost them afterwards through the fault of some of his subordinates. He then returned to Fort Fetterman, withdrawing his forces for the present from the field.

Friday, 31. The system of mixed guards by details from all the companies was replaced last night by the detail of an entire company with its officers, the senior being deemed officer of the day. There are at present five companies, so that guard duty will fall to each every fifth night. In consequence of last night's snow storm we remained in camp today.

Saturday, April 1. Marched at 7:15 A. M., soon reaching the Yellowstone, which we followed down to Shield's River, or Twenty-five Yard Creek as it is sometimes called, where we camped at 1:45 P. M., having marched 19 miles. Power's contract train of wagons has been added to our impedimenta. It left Fort Shaw in advance of us, carrying supplies for sixty days, and united with our command at this camp. Passed two occupied places today, Quinn's ranch, in the gap, and the rather extensive establishment at the Yellowstone ferry.

Shield's River received its name from Captain Clark, in 1806, in honor of one of his men. The trappers of early times called it Twenty-five Yard Creek, and it was a famous resort for them, abounding as it did with innumerable beaver. Two reasons are assigned for the name: its width, which *isn't* twenty-five yards, but much less; and the asserted fact that it rises only twenty-five yards from the source of another stream, which I can neither affirm nor deny. Many sharp conflicts occurred here in olden times between the resolute trapper bands that were wont to frequent the locality and the vengeful Blackfeet who then lorded over it. Near by, in 1867, stood Fort Howie, the stockade of the little army of Montana militia called out by Governor Meagher to battle for their homes with the hostile Sioux, but restrained by the general Government from the merciless campaign they contemplated. Remains of the stockade still exist, and the embankment and ditch are good in this dry climate for a generation or more.

Sunday, 2. Broke camp at 6:30 A. M. The footmen marched by a cut-off near the river, while I followed the road with my detachment as guard to the train. The former reached the camping-ground on the Yellowstone at 11:15 A. M., but the train did not come up until 1:30. Distance traveled by the train, with which the odometer went, seventeen miles, the cut-off taken by the footmen being two or three miles shorter.

Two miles from camp are Dr. Hunter's Warm Springs, which I visited. Found the water very hot, but did not learn the temperature nor the mineral constituents, though sulphur evidently predominates. Gypsum is abundant in this neighborhood. Dr. Hunter's family is now at the Springs, but full of dread of the Sioux. His house is, in the summer season, something of a resort for the afflicted, but the Sioux frequently appear in the vicinity, and once attacked the house—facts which do not attract custom. The springs pour out a copious stream of steaming water, and the day will come when the property will be very valuable.

Last night the sentinels were posted around the camp in groups of three, all lying down but only one required to remain awake at a time. Instead of challenging, the sentinel is directed to whistle to anyone approaching his post and fire upon him if he receives no reply. It is an abominable system, more dangerous to ourselves than to the enemy; and seems to be based upon the fallacy that an Indian will have more compunction about putting an arrow into a whistler than a man who talks out in his mother tongue. As we draw near the dangerous ground, we are dropping into the methods that are to govern our conduct during the campaign. Among these are the groups of three and the whistling.

Monday, 3. Marched at 6:15 A.M., and reached the ford within a few miles. The Yellowstone at this point is about one hundred yards broad and flows with a swift current, but is shallow enough at this season to ford with ease. All the men who could find a place on the wagons were carried over in this manner, and the mounted detachment brought over the remainder, the horses being sent back several times. The crossing occupied only twenty minutes and was effected without mishap, all of which was very creditable to Major Freeman's management. All being over, we resumed the march down the Yellowstone, and, crossing the Big Boulder, a considerable tributary of the former, camped on its right bank at 12:15 P.M. after a march of sixteen miles. The latter part of the march was made through a blinding snowstorm, the snow melting as it fell. It turned quite cold towards night, and was very severe on the animals and the poor fellows of Company A who were exposed in the open air on the wet ground in groups of three. Before the camp was formed, the mounted detachment scouted the surrounding country, and as a further precaution the train was corralled, the troops being disposed on its exterior in a position suitable for defense. The Big Boulder derives its name from the profusion of large round stones with which its channel is filled.

Tuesday, 4. Three inches of snow on the ground this morning, and weather threatening; but nevertheless we marched at 6:45 A.M., following down the valley of the Yellowstone. A cold wind and the bad condition of the road rendered the marching difficult, and after advancing only nine miles camp was formed at 10:15 A.M., upon Big Deer Creek, about a mile from the Yellowstone. A courier came up with us, reporting General Gibbon with the cavalry encamped this evening upon Shield's River. They left Fort Ellis on the first of April and have thus been four days making a distance of thirty miles. This slow progress is attributable to the bad condition of the road over the divide and the snow storm of yesterday, which was more severe near the mountains. The General has changed his plan of operations in consequence of the news received from General Crook. As it is feared that the Indians defeated by him will endeavor to escape toward the north, we are now to keep on down the Yellowstone with a view to intercepting them, instead of turning off toward Fort C. F. Smith[8] as originally planned. The depot at the Crow agency is now of no use, and the stores will be removed to the north bank of the Yellowstone.

Wednesday, 5. Marched at 6:15 A.M. At Bridger's Creek we found a considerable number of white men, with wagons and camp equipage, rendezvousing for the purpose of proceeding to the new gold mines in the Black Hills. We then left the road leading to the Crow agency on Rosebud Creek, or Stillwater, as it is usually called, which we had been following, and continued on down the valley of the Yellowstone by a dim trail that has been little traveled, camping on the river bank at 11:10 A.M., having marched fourteen miles. Most of the timber we have passed today, though still standing, is dead from the effects of fire.

Bridger's Creek is named after the celebrated James Bridger, identified for fifty years with the Great West; but it had an earlier name conferred upon it by the old-time trappers commemorating a most disastrous episode in the early history of this Territory. That name is Emmill's Creek, and as the circumstances that gave rise to it have, I believe, never appeared in print and are but little known, I will take this occasion to place them on record.

AN INDIAN MASSACRE

When the war of 1812 wrought the dissolution of the Missouri Fur Company, a lull fell upon the fur trade of the upper Missouri that lasted for several years. But at length, in the year 1819, an expedition left St. Louis, consisting of about twenty trappers led by Emmill and Jones, the former a native of Chambersburg, Pennsylvania, the latter of unknown origin.

[8] On the Big Horn River, south of present Xavier, Montana.—E. I. S.

They ascended the Missouri, and then all trace of them was lost, and as time passed by without bringing any tidings of them, it became certain that they had perished, but how, when, and where was a mystery that seemed destined never to be solved, and never would have been but for the light thrown upon it by Indian tradition. It appears from this that they followed the Yellowstone River nearly to its source, trapped successfully—accumulating a large quantity of furs —and then commenced their return. But they had been observed by a superior force of Blood Indians—a branch of the Blackfoot nation—who followed them until an opportunity occurred to effect their surprise, when they massacred the entire party and captured their furs, arms and other effects. A Blood Indian who participated in the fight communicated these particulars to Major Culbertson,[9] of the American Fur Company, some twenty years afterward, from whom I received them as well as many other valuable and interesting facts in the early history of this portion of the West. The story became current among the trappers of those times, and, either from remains that they found or from some other cause, they fixed upon the mouth of this stream as the scene of the disaster and conferred upon it in memory of the leader of the ill-fated band, the name of Emmill's Creek. It is a pity that it was ever replaced. Is it too late yet to save it from disuse?

AN INTERESTING INCIDENT

As one descends the Yellowstone, just before reaching Emmill's Creek, he will pass under a perpendicular wall of rock of no considerable height but crowded well in toward the river so as to compress the valley into a narrow space. Ten years ago there might have been seen at its base two graves,

[9] Alexander Culbertson.—E. I. S.

to which, happening to camp then in the vicinity, I made a pilgrimage, but I did not seek them today, and do not know whether they are still discernible or not. They are connected with an interesting incident that the future inhabitants of this region will perhaps thank me for rescuing from oblivion by its introduction here. In the summer of 1866, just after the establishment of Forts Phil Kearny and C. F. Smith on the new route to Montana known as the Bozeman Trail,[10] and while this whole route was the scene of Indian hostility—surprises, attacks, battles, and massacres crowding close on one another's heels—, an old man and his son appeared one day at the former post en route to Montana. It was considered almost certain death for anyone to expose himself in a defenseless condition on any part of this route, and it excited great astonishment that these two venturesome travelers, without other company as they were, had been permitted to traverse some two hundred miles of it unharmed. When remonstrated with upon the folly of such hazardous exposure, the old man replied that he was a believer in fate, that if he was destined to be killed by savages, it was useless to try to evade his destiny, and that if he was not, there could be no danger in his proceeding as he had. The young man had imbibed his father's doctrines in this respect, and citing their almost miraculous preservation thus far, they drew from it an argument in defense of their theory that it was useless to combat, and in spite of all admonition and advice they stubbornly proceeded on their way.

As hostile Sioux appeared almost daily on the route, it was not supposed that they would ever reach Fort C. F. Smith alive; but they did, and encouraged by their impunity, were

10 Named for John M. Bozeman, it provided a "short cut" from the Oregon Trail to the Montana mines. It ran directly through the choice hunting grounds of the Sioux.—E. I. S.

less disposed than ever to be governed by the dictates of common prudence or listen to reason, especially as they had now left the most dangerous country behind. After leaving Fort C. F. Smith, they had to journey about two hundred miles before reaching another white habitation; but they pressed on with blind confidence, and daily drew near to their destination without interruption or mishap.

At length they arrived in the neighborhood of this rock, less than eighty miles from the settlements, and within the limits of the country of the friendly Crows. The danger seemed wholly past, and if the conversation of the travelers could be known, it would probably appear that, as they thus drew near to a place of safety, the old gentleman now and again drew powerful arguments from the immunity they had enjoyed for the confirmation of his son's faith in the doctrine that had governed his own life and that they amused themselves greatly over the apprehension of those who had counseled them against incurring such risks.

But here by the decree of fate they were destined to die, or pay the penalty of their folly and foolhardiness. They fell into an ambuscade of Sioux, and were both killed. Their bodies were found not long afterward and buried near the foot of this rock. There are probably men now resident in Montana who assisted at their burial, as it was effected, if my memory is not a fault, by a party connected with an emigrant train.

Thursday, 6. Marched at 6:10 A. M., passing down the valley, which gradually narrowed and finally ran out—or rather, shifted to the opposite bank of the stream. Here we were compelled to ford and follow down the other bank, crossing without difficulty, in the same manner as before described, and camping at 10:55 A. M., after a march of twelve miles.

The day was beautiful, and soon after the tents were pitched and the camp settled the river bank was thronged with fishermen in gum boots or bare legs seeking to ensnare the finny inhabitants of the stream. Many of the officers joined in the sport, which was very successful, resulting in the taking of at least two hundred pounds of trout that afternoon. Irving has said in *Astoria* that there are no trout in the streams on the eastern slope of the Rocky Mountains, whereas they abound. Many of the smaller streams are alive with them, they are caught in favored portions of the Missouri, and the upper Yellowstone teems with them. It has been said that Yellowstone trout are wormy and unfit to eat, but those caught today, and throughout this campaign, were excellent. Wormy trout have been caught, it is true, but there were probably exceptional causes operating to render them so, as experience has shown that they are generally good.

A Description of the Yellowstone

At the point we struck the Yellowstone, on the first inst., it has just emerged from a deep cut through a lofty chain of the Rocky Mountains, from which point to its junction with the Missouri it traverses an elevated plain, flowing through a valley varying in width from a few hundred yards to a mile or more. The valley is generally bordered with steep bluffs of mingled rock and clay, varying in height from a few score to some hundreds of feet, but the bluffs occasionally give way to a succession of round wooded knolls or a grassy slope of gradual ascent. Sometimes the river cuts through the center of its valley so as to leave a portion on either side, but usually it sweeps across from side to side, leaving the entire valley on one hand and on the other washing the base of the bluffs. The valley is for the most part destitute of timber, but generally well clothed with grass springing out of an excellent soil, though places are not wanting that have been usurped by sage-brush and prickly pear. Considerable timber is met with, however, and groves of greater or lesser extent are scattered along the margin of the stream, in some cases covering hundreds of acres. The timber is mainly cotton-wood, but in some places is interspersed with ash, willow and box-elder. The timber on the bluffs is mainly dwarf pine and fir. The river flows with a rapid current and occasionally breaks into rapids, none of which are difficult to traverse when the water is sufficiently high, and may be run with a small boat with safety at any time. The river begins to rise in April, and reaches its highest point in June, subsiding throughout July and reaching low-water mark in August. The breadth of the stream varies but ranges generally between one hundred and three hundred yards.

Friday, 7. Remained in camp today, officers and men fishing and securing some three hundred pounds of trout. At 3 P.M. General Gibbon and staff arrived, accompanied by Major Brisbin, who commands the cavalry. The cavalry camp tonight at the ford, four miles above. General Gibbon this morning sent word to the Crow agency that he wished to meet the Crows in council at that place. He also requested Mitch Bouyer, a noted guide, to report to him at our camp, designing to employ him to accompany the command if mutually satisfactory.

Saturday, 8. The cavalry came up about 10 A.M., and went into camp about a mile lower down the valley. Mitch Bouyer arrived this morning from the Crow agency and brought word that the Crows were waiting to see the General, who thereupon took my detachment as escort and set out for the agency. We left camp just as the cavalry arrived, the General being accompanied by Major Brisbin, Captain Freeman, and Lieutenant Burnett. Our course led us past Countryman's ranch, a couple of miles below the camp, the last occupied house on the Yellowstone. It is a trading establishment, whisky being the principal commodity, and the customers being Crow Indians. Here we forded the Yellowstone and followed up the valley of Rosebud Creek (or Stillwater Fork, as it is usually called), reaching the agency after a disagreeable ride of eighteen miles, most of the way through a storm of wet snow. We were hospitably received by Mr. Clapp, the agent for the Crows, who provided quarters for officers and men and stabling for our horses. We found here Company E, of our regiment, which marched from Camp Baker in advance of us (March 14) to form part of the expedition, and came on from Fort Ellis to this point in charge of a train of twenty-eight wagons bearing part of our supplies (100,000 lbs.). It is commanded by Captain Clifford and is accompanied by Lieutenant Young. He arrived here April 1, unloaded his train, stored his supplies in the agency ware-rooms, and has been lying here awaiting our arrival.

The agency buildings are well-built structures of adobe, or sun-dried brick, and are so arranged that, with the addition of a heavy plank wall, they enclose a square space of considerable extent. They occupy an elevated plateau overlooking the valley, and the place would be quite defensible against an Indian attack. It is said to have cost only $40,000, and, if true, the money has been more honestly expended than is customary in the Indian Bureau. But the location of the agency is objectionable, as there is very little arable land near it and the close proximity of the lofty Rocky Mountains renders the climate subject to vicissitudes of frost and snow that unfit it for agricultural attempts. At the present time the Crows are gathered here in large numbers to receive their annuities, their white lodges dotting the plain and gleaming through the trees, while their thousands of horses range the surrounding hills. A principal object of the General's visit is to enlist twenty-five Crow warriors as scouts for the ensuing campaign, and a council with the principal men is announced for tomorrow, when the subject will be introduced.

A queer case of exchange of names occurs in the nomenclature of the Stillwater Fork and Rosebud Creek. These names are designed to be an interpretation of the Indian originals, and at first they were rightly applied, that is, the main stream was originally called Rosebud Creek, and the east branch, on which the agency stands, Stillwater Fork. By some hocus-pocus they have become exactly reversed, and everybody now calls the main stream Stillwater. The Indians called the right, or east branch, or rather a portion of it, Stillwater on account of the numerous beaver dams near its source which formerly converted the otherwise impetuous stream into a series of placid pools.

COUNCIL WITH THE CROWS

Saturday, 9. Toward 10 o'clock A. M., the head men of the Mountain Crows began to assemble in a room provided by Mr. Clapp for the holding of the council, and at half-past ten the council opened. General Gibbon and the military officers and gentlemen of the agency occupied one end of the room, Lieutenant Burnett and myself, selected to report the proceedings, sat at a table in their front, with the interpreter Pierre Shane[11] standing near, while the remainder of the room was occupied by the chiefs and head men and the riff-raff of

[11] This man's name is spelled in several ways: Chene, Chane, Chienne, Shane. He was employed as the interpreter at the agency. Lieutenant Bradley is apparently somewhat prejudiced against him.—E. I. S.

the whites, seated on benches provided for the purpose. Having enjoyed no experience as a fashion reporter I shall not attempt to describe the dress of the savages, but will say in passing that there was very little display of finery. Among the principal men were Blackfoot, Tin Belly, Iron Bull, Bull-that-goes-hunting, Show-his-face, Medicine Wolf, Old Onion, Mountain Pocket, Crane-in-the-sky, Sees-all-over-the-land, One Feather, Spotted Horse, Long Snake, Frog, Small Beard, Curly, Shot-in-the-jaw, White Forehead, Old Crow, Old Dog, White Mouth, and Crazy Head. Of these, Bull-that-goes-hunting has the largest number of personal followers, but Blackfoot is reported to have the most influence.

The chiefs having come forward and shaken hands all around, Mr. Clapp said: "General Gibbon, commanding the Military District and the expedition against the Sioux is here to talk with the chiefs and principal soldiers."

General Gibbon—"I have come down here to make war on the Sioux. The Sioux are your enemy and ours. For a long while they have been killing white men and killing Crows. I am going to punish the Sioux for making war upon the white man. If the Crows want to make war upon the Sioux, now is their time. If they want to drive them from their country and prevent them from sending war parties into their country to murder their men, now is their time. If they want to get revenge for the Crows that have fallen, to get revenge for the killing of such men as the gallant soldier, Long Horse, now is their time.

"White men and red men make war in a different way. The white man goes through the country with his head down and sees nothing. The red man keeps his eyes open and can see better than a white man. Now, I want some young warriors of the Crow tribe to go along with me, who will use their eyes and tell me what they see. I don't want men who will be willing to ride along with my men and stay with the wagons, —I have plenty of those. I want young, active, brave men, who will be my eyes. I want twenty-five such men; men who will find out where the Sioux are so that I can go after them. They will be soldiers of the Government, get soldier's pay and soldier's food, and, when I come back, will come back with me and join their tribe again."

The General resumed his seat, and for some time the chiefs sat silent with bowed heads. At length the General informed them that he was ready to hear what they had to say.

Old Crow—"You have said what you had to say; don't be too fast! We are studying within ourselves and will talk after awhile."

White Mouth—"The old man [meaning General Gibbon] is only talking. You have already been down below, our young men went with you, and you turned back after awhile without doing anything. We are afraid that you will do it again."

General Gibbon—"General Brisbin went down suddenly, in the middle of winter, for one thing only—to bring those white men back from Fort Pease. He went down expecting to fight the Sioux if any of them interfered with getting those men away. He went down there and brought the men back. He went in such a hurry that he did not carry provisions enough to stay any length of time. There was no grass to feed his animals. Now there is grass—or will be shortly, and we have men enough and provisions enough to go down there and stay as long as we please. As long as there are any Sioux down there to fight, we will stay. If the Crows will only let us know, or we can find out in any way where the Sioux are, we will stay."

Blackfoot then requested that what he had to say be not interpreted, as they were going to confer among themselves. He then spoke for some time in an animated manner, with impressive gestures, receiving frequent expressions of approval from his native audience. In air and fluency of speech he appeared the orator. Having thus sounded the opinions of his brother chiefs, Blackfoot came forward, shook hands with the General and gentlemen with him, returned to his place, gathered his robe about him leaving one arm exposed and free, and with easy dignity and grace, spoke as follows:

"Perhaps we are a foolish people, but I am going to tell you truly what we think—our way of doing things, what is in our hearts. The Great Spirit knows me, he looks down upon me, he sees me and knows what I feel. I love the white man, I hold on to the hand of the white man with true love for him.

"The white people want us to assist them. I do not know the way of the whites, my people do not know their ways. The land we tread belongs to us, and we want our children always to dwell in it. All other Indian tribes do evil to the whites, but I and my people hold fast to them with love. We want our reservation to be large, we want to go on eating buffalo, and so we hold fast to the whites. I am telling the truth to the white chief. I am a poor man and we are a poor people. I am not ashamed to tell my friends so, the white people, the soldiers, the Great Father at Washington. The Great Spirit knows that I am speaking truth. The soldiers at Fort Ellis are my friends. Are you from Fort Ellis?

"Our young men are before you, but they will not listen to what I say. If you want them to go with you, I would like them to go; but if I tell them to go they will not obey. But should they go, they will want white men with them who can speak their language. It will be well to have such men along. When you tell me the truth, it remains in my heart— I will not forget it; when you speak falsely, I remember that also. I have something to say to you and the Great Father. We are not given enough flour and beef. I want to say this to you and to Mr. Clapp. You ask for some of our young men. If they go, it is right; but if they are unwilling to go, I can not compel them. But they ought to go."

General Gibbon—"I want to hear now from such men as want to get scalps, as want to go to war."

Mr. Clapp—"Some time ago the war widows appeared before the chiefs naked and bleeding from the wounds they had given themselves in their grief, and besought them for revenge. Some of the young men promised to revenge them that they might paint themselves black and cease to mourn. Now is the time for them to get that revenge."

General Gibbon—"I want to hear now from some of the fighting men, such men as Crazy Head, Spotted Horse—men that want to go to war."

Mountain Pocket—"I have fought the Sioux till I am tired. You want to fight now—I'll let you go alone."

General Gibbon—"I'd rather have nobody than an unwilling soldier."

Old Crow came forward and shook hands.

General Gibbon—"This is the man I want to hear talk."

Old Crow—"I have heard that you are going to fight the Sioux. My heart is undecided—I must say that. We love each other, we are like each other. But if we go with you, you might kill some of us if a fight should take place, thinking we were Sioux."

General Gibbon—I am going to have all of my Indian soldiers marked with a red band around the arm."

Old Crow—I am a warrior, I led a party, I went to war, I found a camp, I told the young men to charge. I have done so many times. I always do what I set out to do. If you go and find the Sioux and don't want to fight and tie the young men down, they would cry and break loose and go straight and get killed—and that would be bad. You had better go alone."

General Gibbon—"There is always danger in going to war. Men usually go to war thinking that they may be killed. Men who want to sleep in their teepes every night don't want to go to war. That kind of warriors want to have their squaws in their teepes when they go to war. We don't go that way, we don't want anybody who goes to war that way.

"I have heard several of you talk, the talk all seems to be one way. Now I want to hear from the other side. If any of you want to go to war, I want to hear from you. If not there is an end of it."

Iron Bull (first shaking hands)—"I want to know what route you are going to take."

General Gibbon—"I am going after Indians—never mind which route."

Iron Bull—"When this agency was established, there were in succession several agents for the Crows. We begged them all to take pity on us and help us fight the Sioux. They would not, so we went and fought them alone, though there were not many of us. You say the Sioux are your enemies; so, too, are they mine. You tell us that you are hunting the Sioux, that you have your way of doing it; so, too, have we our way of going to war. If our young men seek the Sioux, they travel night and day till they find them; then they do what they went to do and return. In any other way nothing could be done. You have not told us how long you are going to be gone. If our young men go with you, you will put white men's clothes on them."

General Gibbon—"I shall only give them the strip of red."

Old Crow—"If you take some of the Crows along with you and you find a camp of Sioux and have a fight, I would like to have you send our young men back to see us afterwards. We see each other—we are here together. You tell me what you want with me; I will now tell you what I want with you.

If the Crows go with you, and they find a camp, they will bark like a dog. Will you then jump on the camp and fight right there?"

General Gibbon—"That is what we want."

Old Crow—"That is good. Be patient, do not hurry us. You have told us what you want; now let us hold a council among ourselves and see who will go with you and who will not."

General Gibbon—"I am waiting; I will be here two days."

Old Crow—"That will be enough. The Sioux are a very strong people, a very brave people. Our scouts report to the chief where the camp is, and tell him to get up and go to the camp. Will you believe what the young men tell you? When we go to war, we generally send out a scouting party. If they find a camp they bark like a wolf."

General Gibbon—"I'll believe them if I find they tell the truth."

Old Crow—"They will not lie to you."

Adada a hush—"I will go with you if you go where the Sioux are, but will turn back if you go the wrong way. I will go to the Powder River country."

General Gibbon—"General Crook is there now with plenty of soldiers fighting the Sioux. That is where we want to go."

Adada a hush—"All these men [pointing at the Crow chiefs] talk to you in a way that I don't understand. I don't know what to make of such men."

General Gibbon—"I don't either."

Adada a hush—"When I find where the different bands of Crows are going to camp this summer, I will jump on my horse and go with you. Maybe I can get one or two men to go with you. I don't understand your language. I would like to have some Crows to associate and talk with. We may be gone a long time, and I would become lonesome if alone."

General Gibbon—"We want more. Try to make up a party

to go with us. Tell all the Indians that this is the only man that has shown any disposition to go with us. I don't want any one to go unwillingly. I don't want the Crows to do my fighting—I'll do that myself."

Blackfoot—"You have told us that you were done speaking. Wait awhile, let us think."

Adada a hush—"I have one thing to ask if I get on my horse to go to war. Will you do it?"

General Gibbon—"We can't answer till we hear what it is; we will do it if we can."

Adada a hush—"These people are poor, there is no game, no buffalo. When I get on my horse, will you give them some ammunition to kill game?" (Grunts of approbation from the Crows.)

General Gibbon—"Gen. Clapp is the one to give them ammunition; I have none but for my own use. I will give those who stay behind nothing. I will give all to those who go along."

The Crow speakers then began to make complaints about their rations and agent, and requested the General to intercede for them with the Great Father when, finding that nothing could be gained by further conference, the General invited them to talk over his proposition among themselves and let him know in the evening what they would do, and then withdrew. Thereupon the Indians dispersed, and the council, after a session of about two hours, was at an end.

I have been thus full in my report of its proceedings because it affords an excellent illustration of many prominent traits in the Indian character. Not least among these, it will be noticed by the discriminating reader, is extreme distrust of the white race and its promises to them. Nor did we get through this campaign without unfortunately affording some further grounds for this distrust, as will be seen. The only good object effected by the council was to advertise our purpose among the Crows, and toward evening quite a number of the young men offered their services. We are assured that we shall easily fill up the complement in spite of the cold water cast upon our efforts by the "coffee-coolers," as the shiftless, superannuated loungers about camp are very aptly termed. As Blackfoot remarked, the commands or desires of the chiefs avail little in matters of this kind. The young men settle the question for themselves, and will go or stay as they individually prefer. Captain Clifford marched with his company in the afternoon to join the command.

Blackfoot, the principal orator today, was much more brief in his remarks than he is wont to be, being noted for long harangues and reputed eloquent. Perhaps from the incompetency of the interpreter his speech of today does not do him especial credit. The interpreter is a Frenchman, speaking exceedingly broken English, a fair illustration of which is that once in the course of his interpretation he alluded to God Almighty as "Godulammity." The Earl of Dunraven was very favorably impressed with Blackfoot, and after quoting a number of his more eloquent strains thus says of him:

"Blackfoot may fairly be regarded as a representative man. Superior to the mass of Red Indians, he is a good specimen of the ruling class among them. Endowed in no slight degree with the gift of eloquence, and as the preceding quotations sufficiently testify, provided with a sharp tongue to give utterance to the suggestions of a keen and caustic wit, he is one of many of his race who, had they been properly directed, might have exerted their well-merited influence in the improvement of the condition of their tribe. To call such a man a mere savage and to assert that his race are irreclaimable barbarians who should no longer be allowed to cumber the ground, is as untruthful as it is absurd."[12]

In the afternoon we were treated to the spectacle of a dance by an association among the Crows known as the Foxes. There is a rival society called the Redsticks, and the members of each society make it their business during a certain period of the year to try to seduce the wives of their rivals. A Fox had recently accomplished this feat, and the dance was given in his honor by his brother Foxes, the woman being paraded on horseback—a target for the praises of the Foxes and the gibes of the Redsticks, who had gathered in force to sneer at their rivals and blacken the character of the betrayed one. The lovely one who had stooped to folly seemed untroubled by either poignant grief or melancholy, but on the contrary bore herself with the utmost self-possession and unconcern. She appeared to be about eighteen years old, and will henceforth belong to the Fox who won her from her proper lord. About sixty persons mingled in the dance, all gaudily attired, and what with the drums and rattles and other paraphernalia it was a stirring affair.

Monday, April 10. The General has, very much to my satisfaction, given me the command of the Crow scouts. I completed the desired number of enlistments today, swore them in on the point of a knife—said to be a binding oath among them—and uniformed them with a band of red squaw-cloth about six inches wide, which they are to wear on the left arm above the elbow. This ceremony ended, they desired General Gibbon and myself to take an oath to believe all they should tell us and do as they wanted us to do—rather a preposterous proposition which they retired from upon our swearing to see them furnished with the same pay, rations, and allowances as were received by white soldiers. The detachment consists of

12 *The Great Divide.*

twenty-three Crow Indians and two squaw-men—LeForgey[13] and Bravo—who have lived among the Crows for several years and acquired their language, and therefore will be very useful as interpreters. The warriors are mostly young men of less than thirty years of age, but two are veterans of middle age and two more, old men over sixty, who are expected to do little service beyond giving the young fellows the benefit of their encouragement and advice. They furnish their own arms, all carrying good breech-loaders except two, one of whom has only a revolver and the other a bow and arrows.

Lieutenant Jacobs arrived today from the camp, bringing a train to remove the supplies delivered here by the contract train. He is accompanied as escort by a detachment of the 2nd Cavalry, commanded by Lieutenant McClernand. Before night the stores were all loaded and the train packed ready to return tomorrow. A snow storm set in toward evening, the wet flakes falling rapidly.

Tuesday, 11. About eighteen inches of snow on the ground this morning, but as the storm continued, it was feared we would be completely snowed in unless we extricated ourselves at once, and it was decided to move in spite of the prospect of a hard pull. Toward 9 o'clock A.M. we were all in motion; the General, Jacobs with his train, McClernand with his detachment, and myself with mine. We followed down the Stillwater valley, and as we receded from the mountains found the storm less violent and the snow less deep, till, on reaching the Yellowstone valley, there were but two or three inches and the weather was clear. Lost two mules in crossing the Yellowstone. Found that the command had, on the ninth inst., changed camp, moving down the Yellowstone fifteen

---

[13] This was Thomas H. LeForge. His story is well told by Thomas B. Marquis, *Memoirs of a White Crow Indian* (New York, Century Company, 1928).—E. I. S.

miles, the cavalry and infantry camping for the first time together. The command is now, with the exception of the Crows scouts who will join tomorrow, all together and composed as it is likely to remain throughout the campaign. It consists of six companies of the 7th Infantry, commanded by Captain Freeman, and numbering 13 officers and 220 men, and four companies of the 2nd Cavalry, commanded by Major Brisbin, numbering 10 officers and 185 men. The entire force is under command of Col. John Gibbon, 7th Infantry, and is accompanied by a twelve-pound Napoleon gun and two Gatling guns, calibre .50, all under charge of Lieutenant Woodruff and designed to be served by a detail from the infantry. As for transportation, the force is provided with a train of twenty-four government and twelve contract wagons, the whole number of noncombatants amounting to about twenty men, who in case of necessity will constitute a fair reserve. Dr. Paulding accompanied the cavalry from Fort Ellis, and will be the surgeon of the expedition.

Elsewhere may be found a detailed statement of the strength of the command, which here may be summarized as follows:

General Gibbon and staff..... 3 officers
Infantry battalion .... 13 officers, 220 men.
Cavalry battalion .... 10 officers, 186 men.
Non-combatant .... 1 officer, 20 men.
      Total .... 27 officers, 426 men.

Wednesday, 12. Passed the day in camp preparing for an advance tomorrow. The quantity of stores on hand being in excess of our means of transportation, a temporary depot is to be established here for the surplus, Company A, 7th Infantry (Captain Logan) remaining in charge of it. One of the

Gatling guns will be left with them. Lieutenant Jacobs occupied the day in sorting the supplies and reloading the train, and the company commanders in getting their companies in trim. Bravo came up toward evening with most of the Crow scouts, accompanied by a number of their friends whose presence we had not bargained for. In the evening they entertained the boys with songs accompanied with a thumping of a buffalo robe spread before them—a mystic ceremony termed "making medicine"; that is to say, conjuring for good luck. They were in danger of pushing their incantations into the "wee sma' hours" of the night, but, thinking it best to begin with them at once as I mean to continue, I explained to them the mystery of "taps" and got them quieted down so as not to interfere much with the general repose of the camp.

Thursday, 13. The command marched at 7:15 A.M., Company A, according to programme remaining behind. The remainder of the scouts, except LeForgey and one Crow, came up early in the morning. My command, consisting of the mounted infantry detachment and the Crows, has been assigned the permanent duty of scouting in advance of the column when in march. I sent Bravo with ten scouts ahead early in the morning and followed with the mounted detachment and the remainder of the scouts in time to precede the column a few miles. Route today down the valley of the Yellowstone; camped at 3 P.M., having marched 11.8 miles. No Sioux sign. Had no interpreter with me today, and the Crows took advantage of my inability to give them orders and hung around the column instead of remaining in advance with my detachment. LeForgey, very much to my satisfaction, arrived just as we went into camp, and I shall now be able to keep one interpreter with me and have the best of these slippery Crows, who are now all with me.

Friday, 14. The mounted detachment moved out about 6

A. M., the command following at 7. The Crows did excellent scouting today, scouring the country for a breadth of ten or twelve miles and holding themselves well in front. If allowed, they would be mere camp loafers, but if urged and looked after, they will do good work. No sign of Sioux yet; but the scouts found a camp of five white men engaged in hunting and trapping. Advanced 14.2 miles and camped at 2 P.M. in the Yellowstone valley, about a mile and a half above the point attained last summer by the steamer "Josephine," Captain Grant Marsh,[14] the highest ascent of the river yet achieved.

Saturday, 15. Marched at 6:45 A.M., mounted detachment and scouts in the advance following down the valley across what is known as the Clark's Fork Bottom, so-called because the stream of that name enters the Yellowstone within its limits. On our left the bluffs rose perpendicularly nearly two hundred feet, being crowned with a wall of rock so steep and unbroken that within a distance of several miles it is said to afford only one place of descent. From its appearance this story seems very probable. At the lower end of the bottom the bluffs crowd close on the river, and the road ascends to the plain, which it crosses for some miles, and then by a steep descent regains the valley at Baker's battle-ground. Here at 5 P.M. we went into camp, having marched 17.3 miles.

Indian Hieroglyphics

At the point where the road ascends from the Clark's Fork Bottom, the rocks are lavishly adorned with Indian hieroglyphics, some of them graven deeply in the face of the rock at a considerable height above the ground and in places dif-

---

[14] An almost legendary figure in the history of early navigation on the Missouri and Yellowstone rivers. See Joseph Mills Hanson, *The Conquest of the Missouri* . . . (New York, Murray Hill Books, Inc., 1946).—E. I. S.

ficult of access. I endeavored to learn their meaning from my scouts, but even the oldest of them were unable to tell much about them. They were placed there, they said, by spirits, and every few snows the spirits caused what they had written to disappear and replaced it with something else. The white men, they added, know more than the Crows and ought therefore to be better able than themselves to tell what the spirit meant. It is evident that the inscriptions are of considerable age and that the Crows have entirely lost their meaning, if indeed they ever possessed it. They were probably designed to place on record some unusual occurrence, and with a serious purpose, as the great labor they must have involved forbids the idea of its having been undertaken with trivial intent. Inscriptions of a similar character are scattered all over Crowland, all of which, like these, appear to be quite old. The Crows of the present day attempt nothing of the kind, if indeed they ever practiced such an art. I have become satisfied that the Crows have not occupied this country for more than one hundred years, and it is therefore by no means improbable that the hieroglyphic remains are the work of an earlier tribe.

A Bit of Crow History

The Crows call this locality the 'place of skulls,' and the name commemorates a most disastrous episode in their history. Something less than a hundred years ago the Crows were living in two bands, the greater portion making their home upon the waters of the Powder River, while the smaller band of four hundred lodges, or about four thousand souls, were camped in the lower extremity of the Clark's Fork Bottom, along the base of these bluffs. Here a terrible disease broke out among them, the victims being covered from head to foot with grievous sores. It proved very fatal and destroyed almost the entire band. The plain was covered with the bodies of the dead, and their horses ran wild because there was no one to take care of them. The few who escaped the disease fled to the village on Powder River. The skulls of the victims were subsequently deposited on a natural shelf some two-thirds of the way up the rocky wall, from whence the name— Place of Skulls. It is probable that this destructive malady was the smallpox, as it is a matter of history that about that time it ravaged the country occupied by the tribes along the upper Missouri and in the southern part of British America, reducing their numbers in frightful degree. It was not supposed that the contagion extended to the tribes of this region, but from this tradition it is evident that it did. The tradition terminates with the following romantic incident: There were in the diseased camp two young men who escaped the contagion, and who did not join the few remaining survivors in their flight, but stayed with the sick, doing for them what they could. At last they were alone, and seeing the lodges desolate and their friends, relatives, and countrymen all motionless in death, one said to the other: "It is better to destroy ourselves than die in this manner. We cannot escape—the Great Spirit is angry with the Crows and determined to remove them from the earth. Let us ascend the cliff and, throwing ourselves over, die like brave men." The other consented, and leaping over the precipice they were dashed in pieces on the rocks below.

Today we passed a pile of small stones situated on the ground overlooking the Yellowstone, just below the Place of Skulls. I noticed that some of my Indian scouts paused there, picked up a stone, spit upon it, and cast it upon the pile. Upon inquiry I found that this was done as an act of devotion which they believed would insure them good fortune in their enterprise. They say they have made it a custom for many years, and that the pile of stones was mainly formed in this way. It was however, according to their traditions, originally built as a landmark when they first arrived in this country many generations ago. The same tradition asserts that the Crows left such piles scattered all along the route by which they migrated from the southeast, so that they could find their way back if they ever desired to do so. They assert that even now they can follow these piles all the way from the upper Yellowstone to the Arkansas River, and some of my scouts pointed out a knoll to the southeast where they said the next pile was to be found. I had no opportunity to confirm the truth of this statement, but have been told by white men familiar with the country that to all appearances such a line of stone piles does exist, though in some cases the stones are now dispersed and in others wholly or partially buried in the soil deposited over them by the wind.

Our camping-ground of today derives its name of Baker's battle-ground from an engagement fought here in 1872. No adequate account of the affair has ever appeared in print, and as it is a bit of history worth preserving I shall take this occasion to place it on record as I have gathered it from participants therein. My informants are gentlemen of veracity, and I have been conscientiously careful to state the facts exactly as I received them that I might not do injustice to the reputation of anyone.

BAKER'S BATTLE OF 1872

By the terms of the Charter granted to the Northern Pacific Railroad, the United States Government bound itself to afford all necessary protection against hostile Indians to the parties engaged in the survey of the route and construction of the road. The company desiring in the year 1872 to extend its surveys over the region stretching from the base of the Rocky Mountains to the Missouri River at Bismarck, which was in complete possession of hostile Sioux, called upon the Government for the protection it was pledged to provide. Two surveying parties were to take the field—one to begin at the Missouri River and extend its explorations westward, the other, on the upper Yellowstone and work down that stream till it should meet the eastern corps at the mouth of Powder River. The former was provided with an escort of nearly one thousand men commanded by Colonel David S. Stanley, 22nd Infantry, while to Colonel John Gibbon, 7th Infantry, commanding the District of Montana, was assigned the duty of providing from the troops of his command a suitable force for the protection of the western corps.

For this purpose Companies C, E, G, and I, 7th Infantry, were drawn from Fort Shaw, and companies F, G, H and L, 2nd Cavalry, from Fort Ellis, the whole force, which numbered about four hundred men, being placed under command of Major Eugene M. Baker, 2nd Cavalry. Having marched from their respective posts, they were all assembled at Shield's River on the thirtieth of July, 1872, and, being there joined by Colonel Hayden with his corps of surveyors, began their march down the Yellowstone the following day.

In the meantime a heavy force of Sioux warriors, variously estimated at from eight hundred to one thousand strong, were ascending the river upon a hostile incursion against the Crows; and about the twelfth of August discovered through their scouts that they were in the presence of Baker's command. This unexpected rencontre created a division in their councils, many being anxious to give over their former design and measure powers with the troops, while the more prudent minority were disposed to avoid so hazardous an enterprise and continue their advance on the less prepared and unsuspecting Crows. At length, however, tempted by the large spoils in horses which they hoped by dexterous management to secure at little cost to themselves, they declared in favor of an attack upon the troops, and fixed upon the morning of August fourteenth for carrying the plan into effect.

The troops had now reached and were encamped upon the ground that became the scene of the fight. A party of surveyors escorted by a force of cavalry commanded by Captain Ball had the previous year carried the survey down the Yellowstone valley to the Place of Skulls, and the command having by easy marches reached the field of the summer's work were resting in camp while Col. Hayden completed his arrangements for taking up and continuing the survey. The presence in the neighborhood of two or three Indian dogs had excited some apprehension that there were Indians about, but the general feeling was of confidence and security; and not only were no especial precautions taken by the commander of the force to guard against an attack, but upon the very night fixed for it he permitted himself to become unfitted for the proper performance of his duties by an overindulgence in strong drink.

The camp was pitched upon ground favorable for defense, being located upon the margin of the stream, with a timbered slough sweeping in a semi-circular direction around it so as to form in connection with the river what may be termed an island of two or three score acres area, the whole at long rifle-range from the adjacent bluffs. To have rendered the position wholly secure, however, it would have been necessary so to guard the slough that it could not be occupied by the enemy as a preliminary to their attack; but this was not done. Fortunately it was rather the purpose of the Indians to get possession of the animals of the command with as little fighting as possible than to gain any decisive advantage over the troops, and their plans were laid accordingly. Several hundred warriors were posted close on the lower side of the camp, where they were wholly screened from view by the timber and willows growing in profusion at the lower extremity of the slough, while the remainder of their force was to seek by an attack upon the landward side of the camp to draw the troops in that direction, when the ambushed swarms would burst from their concealment, sweep over the camp, cut loose the horses, throw the troops into confusion by attacking their rear, and at the worst escape with the herd. With such caution and success did they, under cover of the darkness, reconnoiter the camp previous to the attack that they were enabled to steal several saddles out of the tents of a party of prospectors, who had joined the command, while their owners lay within them asleep, cut from their lines and make off with six mules picketed near the tent of the commanding officer, and kill a dog that threatened to betray their presence in the camp.

The guard that night consisted of a mixed detail of cavalry and infantry numbering twenty-six men, commanded by Lieutenant (now Captain) William Logan,[15] 7th Infantry, a brave and sagacious officer, who was of the number that suspected the presence of the Sioux and, having a premonition of the attack, did all that a vigilant officer of the guard could do to avert surprise. His guard was posted on the flank of the camp, away from the river and some three hundred yards distant therefrom, his sentinels covering the camp as far as possible, while the herds of beef cattle and mules of the government and contractor's trains, which had been left out to graze, and held well under cover of the guard upon the island already described, with a squad of herders over them to pre-

---

[15] Killed in the Big Hole Battle, August 9, 1877. See *The Battle of the Big Hole*, by G. O. Shields ("Coquina").—W. E. S.

vent straggling or stampede. The horses of the cavalry were tied at the picket lines within the limits of the camp.

Toward 3 o'clock A. M., of August fourteenth, the officer of the guard made the round of his sentinels and found all quiet, the guard tents and the timber growing along the slough. Soon afterward from the timber at different points along the landward side of the slough the Indians opened fire and advanced upon the island to attempt the capture of the herd. In a moment the boldest of them were mingled with the animals, but the few men posted over the herd stood their ground manfully, opening a rapid fire upon their assailants at close range, and at the same time endeavoring to put the herd in motion toward the corral. The guard was instantly under arms, by judicious management the animals were driven gently to the rear, the Sioux who had sought to stampede them being forced by the fire of the guard to fall back. A few moments sufficed to enable Lieutenant Logan to throw his entire guard between the Sioux and the herd, where deployed as skirmishers and lying down in the long grass the men opened fire upon the moving forms dimly seen before them through the gloom. After the first volley the Sioux maintained a scattering fire, but the unexpectedly hot reception given them by the guard soon caused them to retire from the timber to the open ground beyond, and, within a few moments after the attack began, the ground was cleared of them and their fire had subsided into a few straggling shots.

Meantime the herders conducted the animals to the rear, where without confusion they were driven into the corral and rendered secure, none having been lost, except fifteen head of beef cattle which stubbornly refused to move with the herd and fell into the hands of the Sioux. When the firing began, the citizen prospectors, some twenty in number, seized their arms and took an advanced position on the left of the guard, where with Lieutenant Jacobs at their head they took cover and opened battle on their individual account. The Sioux speedily recovered from their first repulse and returned to the attack, reoccupying the timber and appearing in considerable numbers on the open ground in front of the guard. But the citizens with Lieutenant Jacobs poured in a rapid fire upon their flank while the guard received them firmly in front, handling their breech-loaders with such effect that again the Indians speedily withdrew.

At the first alarm the troops had promptly formed in their company streets and awaited the orders of the officer in command. As soon as the infantry battalion was under arms, Captain Rawn, its commander, reported to Major Baker for orders and found him still in bed, stupefied with drink, skeptical as to the presence of an enemy, and inclined to treat the whole alarm as a groundless fright upon the part of the guard. It was difficult to get any order from him, but at last he directed Captain to Rawn to hold his men in camp; and, disgusted and angry, that officer returned to his command and upon his own responsibility deployed Companies E (Lieut. Reed) and G (Capt. Browning) in line on the lower side of the camp, facing the thicket in which the ambuscade had been formed. Lieutenant Reed occupied the right, with his right flank resting on the stream, and thus posted, the men of both companies lay down in the tall grass. As bullets were flying freely through the camp, the remainder of the command was ordered to lie down in their company streets.

Captain Thompson, officer of the day, had gone to the front to ascertain the cause of alarm, and nearly lost his life by advancing recklessly too far beyond the guard. Finding the attack real, he so reported to the commanding officer, and a re-enforcement of about thirty cavalrymen under Lieutenant Hamilton was sent forward to Logan's support. Captain Rawn at last received tardy orders to deploy his command, and thereupon placed Company C (Lieut. Quinton) in position on the left of the line already formed, and his own company, I, on the left of C, and then by extending intervals to the left caused the four infantry companies to cover about half the front, the citizens and cavalry continuing the line to the left till it enveloped the camp. This deployment was effected within about half an hour after the beginning of the attack.

As yet the Indians ambushed on the lower side of the camp had not betrayed their presence by a sound. It was now growing light, and seeing the movement of the troops toward the point of attack, but ignorant that while it was yet dark two whole companies had taken position directly in their front, they imagined that their stratagem had succeeded, and the way was open to the picket lines where the horses were tied. They began therefore to make their way cautiously forward, but ere they emerged into view Lieutenant Reed discovered the movement in the sudden rustling and swaying of the willows in his front, and promptly swept the covert with his fire, pouring three volleys by company into the timber with the regularity and precision of the drill-ground. This sudden and unlooked for storm of bullets full in their faces filled the Indians with astonishment and dismay. Without waiting to return a shot, they swarmed from the timber like bees and spurred their horses away for the bluffs in headlong flight. As they passed the remainder of the line, Companies C, G, and I also opened fire and completed their utter discomfiture. True to the Indian custom they carried with them their killed and wounded slung across their horses in their front, and Lieutenant Quinton, who occupied a favorable position for observing their movements, counted eighteen thus borne from the field.

The slough with its timber belt was now in possession of

the troops, and afforded them excellent cover from the desultory fire which the Indians maintained for the next three or four hours from the bluffs. After the repulse of the latter from their ambuscade, they attempted no movement of consequence, but remained for the most part gathered in crowds upon the distant bluffs. Occasionally some of the bolder warriors careened on horseback at full speed along the line, a few of whom were wounded for their pains. About 8 o'clock A. M., they suddenly disappeared, and a reconnaissance by Captain Ball's company of cavalry showed them in full retreat. The officers generally were eager to follow them, and Major Baker at one time ordered Captain Rawn to get two of his companies in readiness to move, announcing his determination to take them and two companies of his "busters"—as he was pleased to call the cavalry—and pursue; but he soon forgot all about it or changed his mind. Accounts agree in representing the Indians as greatly demoralized. They afterwards admitted a loss of over forty killed (all but three of whom they carried from the field), and there was also a large number of wounded, probably nearly a hundred in all. They fled with great precipitation, and marked their line of retreat with abandoned effects that would have impeded their flight. A vigorous pursuit, encumbered with dead and wounded as they were, would speedily have brought them to bay, and an energetic commander with his wits about him and such a force at his command would probably have gained a decisive success. Baker's star as an Indian fighter shone out brilliantly on the Marias River in January, 1870,[16] but suffered a great diminution of luster on the Yellowstone in August, 1872. The troops in

[16] This incident is generally known as the "Baker Massacre." In retaliation for the killing of one Malcolm Clark, Baker, with four troops of the Second Cavalry, killed 173 Indians, 53 of whom were women and children. It subsequently developed that they were not of the band which had killed Clark, although both bands were Piegans.—E. I. S.

this engagement suffered a loss of only one killed—Sergeant McLaren, Co. C, 7th Infantry, and three severely wounded—Privates O'Mally, Co. E, 7th Infantry, and Ward, Co. L, and Cox, Co. F, 2nd Cavalry. One of the citizens, Francis, was also wounded and died three days after the engagement.

After this affair the troops continued their march slowly down the north bank of the Yellowstone, the engineers carrying forward their survey; but Engineer Hayden's fears had got the better of him, and he sought an occasion to return. He sounded the opinions of the officers, but found the majority of them in favor of pushing on and satisfied of their ability to take care of themselves. At last, on the twentieth of August, at a point about six miles above Pompey's Pillar, he insisted upon returning or turning off toward the Musselshell, and the latter course was pursued. After surveying across the country to that stream and up its south fork, the expedition finally disbanded on the twenty-fifth of September, the troops returning to their posts. Engineer Hayden, though wholly responsible for the failure to prosecute the survey to Powder River as had been originally designed, afterwards endeavored to shirk it upon the military. Had it been his desire to proceed, there would have been no hesitation on the part of the commander of the troops to accompany him; and the great majority of the officers were eager to go on, to save that command from any suspicion of having been frightened from its purpose by Indian hostility.

Sunday, 16. Lieutenant McClernand being sent forward this morning with a working party to fix the ford, I was ordered to cover him with my detachment and the scouts. Left camp about 6 A. M., crossed the river a couple of miles below, and passing down the opposite bank took a position in the hills below Pryor's River, from which I could overlook the country for miles, and remained there throughout the day. The command broke camp at 9:35 A. M., marched six miles, fording the Yellowstone above Pryor's River, and camped at 3:15 P. M. just below the mouth of the latter stream. Lieutenant Schofield had a narrow escape from drowning in crossing the ford. His horse deviated from the ford, got into deep water, and became unmanageable. In his frantic efforts Lieutenant Schofield was swept from the saddle and left struggling in several feet of water, and, being unable to swim, was submerged, and becoming insensible; would have been inevitably drowned had he not clung to the bridle reins and been dragged ashore by the horse. Toward evening I left my perch in the hills and went to the camp. Still no sign of the Sioux, though the scouts predicted that we should find it about Pryor's River, which, said they, the Sioux continually infest. Two years ago the Crow camp which pitched on this spot was assaulted by several hundred Sioux warriors, and as the Crows were present in strong force, a lively battle ensued, lasting nearly all day and finally terminating in the repulse of the Sioux with severe loss. One of my men picked up a rusty carbine on the field—undoubtedly a relic of the fight.

Monday, 17. Marched at 8 A. M., my detachment in advance. Followed down the Yellowstone valley, crossing Arrow Creek (otherwise Cachewood Creek) in our course, and camped a few hundred yards below Pompey's Pillar[17] at 4 P. M., having marched 15.8 miles. We have been a good deal annoyed by the presence of fourteen Crows who attached themselves to our command and have exerted a bad influence over our scouts, seducing them from their duty and encouraging them in restlessness under the restraint it is necessary to impose. General Gibbon gave them their choice this evening either

---

[17] Named "Pomp's Tower" in honor of Sacajawea's son, this is the most famous landmark on the Yellowstone River.—E. I. S.

to leave the command or make a scout down the river, in the latter case being furnished with three days' rations. They chose the latter, receiving their rations, and left just before dark, accompanied by two of my scouts, who are to return with such information as may be gathered during the scout. "Muggins" Taylor and one of my Crows set off this evening to scout toward the Big Horn.

Tuesday, 18. We passed the day in camp. The Crows were scattered around in different directions, a party being sent some miles back on our trail to ascertain whether we are being dogged by Sioux. All but one returned in the evening without having found any sign. The absentee has taken French leave and connected himself with the volunteers who left camp last night for the down-river scout. Taylor and his companion came in without having seen any sign, though they had advanced quite to the Big Horn. It is pretty evident that the Sioux are not yet about us and are ignorant of our presence here. But in lieu of Sioux the scouts report innumerable buffalo feeding quietly. This is accounted for by some as further proof of the absence of Sioux, but, inasmuch as the Indians often observe such care in their buffalo hunts that the same herd will graze for days in the immediate neighborhood of their camp, though suffering daily loss, it is not in itself conclusive evidence.

Our boys have been busy all day transmitting their names to posterity by carving them in the soft sandstone of Pompey's Pillar. A number of earlier visitors have done so, first among whom was Captain Clark, who, on the occasion of his descent of the Yellowstone in 1806, discovered the rock and gave it its name. "Wm. Clark, July 25, 1806" is the inscription he left behind, and it still appears as distinctly as when graven there seventy years ago. But a cavalry vandal today disfigured the inscription by carving his own name over the letter "K," for which he deserves to be pilloried. When taken to task about it, he is said to have defended himself by saying: "Be Jases, it's a dom lie anyhow, for there wuz niver a white man in this country sivinty years ago." The "Josephine" was the first steamboat to ascend the river thus far, and has left its name inscribed in token thereof. Many of the officers expressed themselves disappointed when they saw the rock, having expected to see a slender shaft rearing itself needle-like above all surrounding objects, whereas in fact the rock is broader than it is high, slopes off gradually on the river side, and is overtopped by the neighboring bluffs of which at one time it formed a part. The name is something of a misnomer, but a reference to the journal of Lewis and Clark will show that they described it fairly.

I am tempted in this connection to ask, why do the books all spell Captain Clark's name with an "e"? In three editions of Lewis and Clark's journal and two of Cass's journal in my possession it is so spelled invariably, while in some other old books it is spelled both ways. Irving and nearly all modern authors spell it with the "e." But it is undoubtedly wrong. Col. Geo. Rogers Clark, his brother, is better treated, his historians always omitted the "e." In the inscription left by Captain Clark on Pompey's Pillar there is no "e," and it seems to have been his habit in all cases so to sign himself.[18]

Wednesday, 19. Marched at 7:30 A. M., route down the valley of the Yellowstone, cavalry and train fording the river twice. Scouted both banks with the Indians and my detach-

---

[18] According to Mrs. Ann Clark Thurston Farrar, the mother of Mrs. S. T. Hauser, of Helena, and a niece of Captain William Clark, the final "e" was used or omitted at the pleasure of the writer. The name is frequently, and probably the more correctly, spelled without it; and this is the way Mr. Jefferson Clark, now of St. Louis, Mo., who is a son of Captain Clark, writes his name. A similar mutation in the spelling of names is illustrated in many other instances beside this.—W.E.S.

ment, the infantry following a rugged game trail over the ridge that forces the road across the stream and thus avoiding the fords. Marched 18.5 miles, and camped at 3:30 P.M. near the river bank. Still no sign of the Sioux.

Thursday, 20. One of the sentinels thought he saw a signal light on the bluffs last night, but the Indians who were sent to investigate it could find no sign of human presence. Marched at 7:30 A.M., my command in the lead. Forded the Yellowstone not far above the mouth of the Big Horn, which stream we passed today. The Yellowstone has been rising for some time, and it was difficult to find a fording place for the train. As it was, the water entered the beds of the wagons, and many of the mounted men caught a plentiful supply in their boots. The road after gaining the left bank of the Yellowstone ascends to an irregular upland, which it traverses for a few miles, regaining the valley about two miles above Fort F. D. Pease and some five miles below the mouth of the Big Horn. At this point we went into camp at 5 P.M., having marched 17.2 miles. The Crows found today fresh tracks of two horses and other fresh horse signs which we at first supposed to indicate the presence of Sioux scouts, but it transpired that there are a couple of wild horses in the neighborhood. So no Sioux yet; but we are getting well into their country, and the scouts are very cautious in their movements.

Fort Pease is in plain view from our camp, and parties from the command visited it this afternoon. The flag is still flying as it was left when abandoned some weeks ago, and the fort itself is untouched. It is evident that the Sioux have not visited it, as there are no traces of their presence, and besides they would have set the place on fire had they been here. A greyhound was found inhabiting it, who has been its solitary occupant for weeks. He was overjoyed to see human beings again.

How he subsisted is a mystery, but probably by hunting rabbits and other small game.

Friday, April 21. Will Logan (son of Capt. Logan), accompanied by a soldier, arrived this morning from the supply camp bearing mail and dispatches. It appears that General Crook has not yet retaken the field and will not before the middle of May, and that General Custer will not start from Fort Abraham Lincoln[19] until about the same time. We were to have acted in conjunction with these forces, but we are now, when well advanced in the Sioux country, left unsupported. General Crook's victory was not so decisive as we have regarded it, while the fighting seems to have demonstrated that there are heavier forces of warriors to encounter than had been counted upon. General Terry fears that the Indians may combine and get the better of us; and we are therefore to cease our advance for the present and remain in this vicinity until further orders, in a state of inactivity unless sure of striking a successful blow. Now for tedious camp life and a long campaign.

In the afternoon the command moved down the river and camped at Fort Pease, whose buildings will make good storehouses for our supplies while we lie here inactive. The train will be unloaded and sent back after the supplies left behind in Captain Logan's charge.

A Sketch of Fort Pease

Fort Pease is built close to the bank of the Yellowstone, and like the majority of the structures of this class is a combination of log buildings and palisades, enclosing a space about two hundred feet square. The buildings and palisades are

---

[19] A few miles below present Mandan, North Dakota. It is now being restored.—E. I. S.

loop-holed on every side, commanding as well the interior as the exterior of the fort. It was built in the spring of 1875 by a colony from Bozeman, who descended the Yellowstone in boats and established themselves here in the expectation that steamboating would soon become a regular feature of the Yellowstone and that this would be an important point on the river. A considerable quantity of goods was accumulated here to meet the demands of the expected trade, and it is said that several farms were located, a town laid out, and other preparations made looking to the carrying on of a thriving colony. The fort was named in honor of F. D. Pease, the leader of the expedition and a principal promoter of the enterprise.

But the times were not propitious and the enterprise was doomed to a troubled life and an early death. The Sioux war broke out, no steamers came to ply on the Yellowstone, no military post was located near by as had been anticipated, and additional settlers did not resort to the vicinity while swarms of hostile Indians did. The Sioux declared unrelenting war upon the fort and its little band of forty men, and night and day beleaguered the place, seeking occasion to ply their murderous work. The life of the garrison became a series of skirmishes, the crack of rifles handled with deadly intent became a familiar sound, and now and then the heavy boom of an iron six-pounder with which the fort was provided roared over the valley, startling the echoes in the neighboring cliffs.

This life of incessant warfare told severely on the little garrison. Many an Indian was made to bite the dust, but six of their own number laid down their lives in the defense, while nine more were suffering from wounds; and as the Indians hung about them in accumulating swarms, the dread apprehension fell on the survivors that they might all perish. Their numbers were now reduced to twenty-eight men, and it was resolved to appeal to the commanding officer of Fort Ellis to send down a force to relieve them and enable them to get out of the country. This resolution was carried into effect, General Terry gave the necessary orders for the movement, and, on the twenty-second of February, 1876, Major Brisbin at the head of four companies of the 2nd Cavalry left Fort Ellis for their release. Prior to his arrival at the fort, the Indians, tiring at the stubborn defense, retired from the vicinity, applauding the courage of the garrison and asserting that they were done with them and that they might now stay as long as they pleased. But the few men left in the fort were glad to accept the opportunity to take safe leave of the scene of so much strife and anxiety, and the fort was abandoned in March.[20] The colors of the fort were left flying where they had so often waved defiance to encircling Sioux, and it was also the design to leave the walls and buildings entire, but a discontented member of the party secretly set one of them on fire, which was burned without injury to the rest. We found the fort in the condition it had been left, and it is evident that the Sioux have not since been in the vicinity and are ignorant of its abandonment. Its history covers a period of less than a year, but teems with incident, and, when written in full with due attention to the instances of thrilling personal adventure enacted around it, will form an interesting and valuable chapter in the records of the western border.

Saturday, 22. Two couriers left Captain Logan's camp on the nineteenth inst., one day before Will Logan, and from

[20] But Peter Koch was later to write, "But when General Brisbin seems to believe that the little garrison at Fort Pease was listening for his bugles, as the garrison at Lucknow listened for the pipes of Havelock, he was never more mistaken in his life." *Contributions to the Historical Society of Montana,* II, (1896), 137.—E. I. S.

JAMES H. BRADLEY
first lieutenant, Seventh U. S. Infantry.

"A BLACKFOOT INDIAN"
from a drawing by Charles Bodmer.

the length of time they were out fears were entertained that they had been intercepted by Sioux or drowned in crossing the river. Four of the Crows were sent back at 1 o'clock this morning to look for them, two of whom have returned. They report having found the trail of the couriers, which turns back up the river at our last camping ground, the tracks indicating that one of them is afoot. The mystery was only deepened by this discovery, but we subsequently learned that one of their horses gave out, when, despairing of being able to overtake the command, they turned back. Of the absent Crows one is sick and the other remains to take care of him. One of the two that returned insists upon taking back the horses and effects of himself and the two absentees, to the end that all three may return to the agency. It is difficult to impress upon these fellows the fact that their act of enlistment imposes the duty of obedience to orders and inhibits that free skurrying to and fro over the country to which they have been accustomed. Four cavalrymen left for Fort Ellis at 1 o'clock A. M., carrying mail. It is dangerous service, as these small parties are exceedingly liable to be cut off by the Sioux. Some of the Crows are each day kept scouting about camp, but have seen no Sioux sign as yet.

Sunday, 23. Captain Freeman, accompanied by Lieutenant Kendrick, left this morning with his company (H, 7th Infantry) in charge of twenty-seven wagons, part of which are to be used in bringing down the supplies left at Logan's camp, the remainder, five in number, to return to Fort Ellis, being discharged contract teams of Power's train. An ambulance, with four mounted men as escort, left with them to bring back the sick Indian, returning in the afternoon. He had recovered and, with his companions, was returning horseback.

Monday, 24. Captain Clifford and Lieutenant Johnson with two men went down the valley hunting this morning, which afforded the camp an excitement and me an opportunity for a scamper. They were sighted by the Crow scouts at some distance below and mistaken for Sioux, whereupon the latter made a tragical rush for our camp to give the alarm. As they appeared in view across the valley running in single file at a lively speed, occasionally deviating from a direct line to describe a small circle indicating that they had seen an enemy, quite an excitement was aroused in the camp. The soldiers gathered in throngs, while the Crows formed in line, shoulder to shoulder, behind a pile of buffalo-chips placed for the purpose and stood there swaying their bodies and singing while the scouts approached. As the leader of the scouts came up, he paused to kick over the pile of buffalo-chips, which was equivalent to a solemn pledge to tell the truth, then sat down surrounded by his fellow Crows and, after resting a minute or two, told what he had seen.

The Crows, full of enthusiasm, rushed after their horses and stripped for a fight; while I got my detachment in the saddle as quickly as possible, and away we went down the valley looking for a brush and hoping to bag a few Sioux. About eight miles down we found the trail of the party seen by the scouts, and behold it was the trail of Captain Clifford and his little hunting party, who, ignorant of the commotion they had innocently aroused, had ridden on to other fields. We returned to camp considerably crest-fallen, and with impaired confidence in the judgment of the Crows.

Companies H (Capt. Ball) and F (Lieut. Roe), 2nd Cavalry, about eighty strong, commanded by the former officer, left this afternoon for a scout up the Big Horn River. They are accompanied as guides by two of my scouts—LeForgey, interpreter, and a Crow, Jack Rabbit Bull.

The men are rendering their stay here as pleasant as possible by raising their beds off the ground, building shades of boughs over their tents, etc. The camp now wears quite a picnic air. Still no sign of Sioux.

Tuesday, 25—Sunday, 30. During these six days we have remained quietly in camp, amusing ourselves as best we could. Hunting parties go out occasionally, but do not procure much game; and fishermen throng the bank, securing a fair return in cat-fish, hickory shad, and suckers. The Crows have kept a look-out around camp, and a party of six made a scout down the river as far as the mouth of the Rosebud River, leaving camp on the twenty-seventh and returning on the thirtieth, finding the country full of buffalo but discovering no sign of the Sioux. Three of the Crows—the same who desired to leave a few days ago—stole away on the twenty-ninth with all their horses and effects and are yet absent. They have undoubtedly deserted. An Indian is a sufficiently lazy creature, but he likes to choose his own time and method of indulgence, and this enforced camp life is very distasteful to the Crows. We received a mail from above on the twenty-eighth.

HISTORICAL SKETCH OF THE CROWS

In my detachment of scouts are two or three old men who are well informed in the traditions of their tribe, and my principal occupation during these days of idleness, and those that subsequently occurred during the campaign, was to collect from them and commit to writing such information as they could give me concerning their people and the region they inhabit. I have also sought similar facts from every other available source, and by these means have made a considerable compilation of Crow history. Inasmuch as they are a very interesting tribe, and have allied themselves with us in this war, and the country in which we are to operate was formerly their home, there seems good reason for introducing here some account of them. I do not think there is a comprehensive sketch of their history in print, and this may serve to supply the lack until a fuller and better account appears. . . .[21]

When the present Crow tribe first became known to white men, it occupied the tract of country stretching from the North Platte River to the Yellowstone along the eastern base of the Rocky Mountains, extending its range as far eastward as the mouth of the Yellowstone and occasionally passing to the northward of that stream into the valley of the Mussel-shell and Judith rivers. It is not certain when the Crows were first visited by white men, but the earliest authenticated visit that has come under my observation is that of John Colter in 1806. He had been a member of Lewis and Clark's party, but, having become enamored of the wild life of the West, procured his discharge and remained in the country with two friends hunting and trapping for a livelihood. Captain Clark passed through their country in descending the Yellowstone in 1806 but encountered no members of the tribe, though it is probable they saw him, as his horses were stolen, the thieves undoubtedly being Crows.

The next year, 1807, Lisa with a numerous party ascended to the mouth of the Big Horn and there built the first trading post located within the limits of Crow-land. He remained there trading with the tribe for nine months, and in 1808 broke up his establishment and returned to St. Louis. In the year 1807 another party of trappers and hunters entered the country from St. Louis, having traveled on horseback by way of the Mandan villages and the Yellowstone valley. They had suffered a defeat from the Blackfeet and were then retreating to the south. Having rested a few days in the Crow camp, they pursued their journey; but one of the number, Edward Rose, remained with the Crows, married one of their women,

21 Ellipsis indicated in original publication of the Journal.—E. I. S.

became a man of great influence among them, and finally lost his life in a conflict with the Arickarees. The next party of white men to enter their country was that of Hunt, a partner with Astor in the Pacific Fur Company, who, in 1811, ascended the Missouri to the Arickaree villages, then crossed overland through the Crow country to the headwaters of Snake River, and proceeded finally to the Pacific at Astoria. All these various parties were received by the Crows in a friendly manner, but their horse-stealing proclivities got for the tribe a bad reputation, and by all the other writers they are pronounced a thieving, lawless, plundering horde.

By the traditions of the tribe it is made to appear that they emigrated from the southeast, and there is good reason for believing that they once dwelt upon the waters of the Gulf of Mexico or along the Atlantic coast in Georgia or South Carolina.[22] The Crows are remarkable for the evidence they present of having at some early period in their history received a considerable admixture of white blood; and one hundred years ago the Cherokee Indians of Georgia had a tradition of having in former times expelled a tribe of *white* Indians from that country, who, they said, fled to the Mississippi and then up the Missouri where they yet dwelt. Among the other evidences of their southeastern origin are traditions that they once dwelt in a land of perpetual summer, where they grew corn, and they possess a lingering dim knowledge of the alligator which could only have been acquired in a southern land. They say that they once dwelt upon a great water so broad that they did not know its extent, and that it was out of this water that the first white men came to them, as well as the first horses they ever saw. This tradition is almost lost, and all their other traditions are vague and indistinct. May not

[22] Lieut. McClernand, who has made some research concerning the tribe, thinks it was Lake Michigan, but I am unable to agree with this view—J. H. B.

this one dimly preserve the remembrance of someone of the Spanish maritime expeditions to the Southern Coast in the sixteenth century?

The last migration of the Crows was made about 125 years ago, say in 1750, from a stream they term the Flint River, where they had dwelt for an indefinite period. By this name is said to be meant the Kansas River, and, from the position they assign to it, that idea is probably correct. Almost all their traditionary history is embraced in the period subsequent to that migration, all of earlier date being caught only in transient gleams. In the year 1724 there resided upon the headwaters of the Kansas River a powerful band of Indians, known to the French by the name of Paducas, who dwelt in several villages and could bring into the field about two thousand men. From this country they suddenly disappeared, and no trace of them has ever been found. Captain Lewis, writing in 1805, says that they appear to have removed to the upper Platte River, and there dispersed into various bands which took different names. The north fork of the Platte was once called the Paducas Fork, probably after this tribe.

I am not yet prepared to assert it as a fact, but I do not hesitate to express it as my conviction that we must seek for the lost Paducas in the present Crows. The Crows, according to their tradition, dwelt upon the headwaters of the Kansas River at the period the Paducas are represented as being there, and migrated to the northwest about the time the Paducas are reported to have disappeared. As Captain Lewis says of the Paducas, the Crows went first to the headwaters of the Platte and rested for a time from their migration upon the north fork of that river, which was formerly called the Paducas Fork. Such a coincidence of time and circumstance would amount to positive proof of their identity as one and the same tribe, but for the element of doubt in the traditions of the Crows. I feel convinced that they are to be relied upon and that I have made correct deductions from them as to the period when the migration took place, but prefer to make additional investigation before committing myself irrevocably to the proposition I have advanced.

But though, while located upon the waters of the North Platte, the Crows (or Paducas) did not disperse into the numerous or petty bands conjectured by Captain Lewis, an important division occurred which marks the real beginning of the present Crow tribe. Dissensions had for a long time existed among them that induced them to divide into two bands, who pitched their camps a little apart. During this state of things a famine arose, and at the season of greatest scarcity a buffalo was killed, over the division of which a quarrel ensued between the two camps and permanent separation was agreed upon. One band went to the northeast, made its home on the Missouri River, and became the Minnetarees or Gros Ventres of the Missouri of the present day, while the other band spread to the northwest and is now known as the Crows. Their differences never led them to war upon each other, and within a few years after the separation they began an interchange of visits that continues, in a reduced degree, to the present day. Not only their traditions but the affinities of tongue prove them allied to each other; and among the Minnetarees, as among the Crows, frequent instances of blue and gray eyes, light hair, and a fair skin prove a former infusion of white blood. This separation of the bands occurred not later than 1775, and possibly a few years earlier.

The Crows, having become a separate tribe, designed extending their migration still farther to the northwest, but, finding themselves confronted by the succession of lofty mountain ranges in Montana and learning from the Nez Percés that the country continued to be rugged and mountainous for a long distance farther on, paused in their advance and occupied the country in which they were found by their first white visitors. Here they suffered from the visitation of the smallpox, already described, by which their numbers were reduced from about one thousand lodges, or ten thousand souls, to six hundred lodges with six thousand souls. They gradually recovered from this depletion of numbers, and about the year 1822 were once more nearly one thousand lodges strong, when there occurred the most terrible calamity that ever befell the tribe, sweeping off in a single day about half their numbers and leaving the survivors impoverished.

In the summer of this year a warlike fever seemed suddenly to have possessed the Crows, and party after party took the field, until eight large bands had gone forth, comprising the greater number of their warriors and the flower of their tribe. While in this condition of comparative defenselessness, the camp was suddenly assailed by a combined force of Sioux and Cheyennes numbering over one thousand men. Panic seized upon the Crows, and with little attempt at resistance they fled in wild confusion over the plain toward the neighboring hills. The Sioux and Cheyennes were mostly mounted, and had only to ride after the fleeing throngs and slay them as they ran. Hundreds were overtaken and killed in the village and hundreds more in the subsequent pursuit, which continued for miles. The plain was literally strewn for a considerable distance with the corpses of men, women, and children; and at last from the very fatigue of killing and satiated with blood, the victors desisted from the pursuit. It had not been a battle but a butchery, and a butchery the most terrible that either in tradition or history has occurred upon the great plains of the Great West. At least five thousand of the Crows had fallen, but that was not all. All their lodges—a thousand in number—all the equipage of their camp, and hundreds of horses had passed into the hands of the victors, who also carried away as captives four hundred young women and children. The Crows in time recovered from the loss of material, but have never regained the numbers they possessed upon the morning of that fatal day.

After the exploration of Lewis and Clark had made known to the world the geography and resources of the West, numerous parties of trappers, traders and travelers found their way hither and the Crows had frequent white visitors. But while the majority of the Indian tribes east of the mountains received such parties with hostility, the Crows preserved toward them peaceful relations, though not hesitating to rob them and drive off their horses when opportunity offered. These acts of unfriendliness were, however, confined in the main to the worse spirits of the tribe, the general sentiment being of friendliness, and their villages ever afforded a place of refuge to the harassed parties of white men who roamed the West. But in the year 1825 a difficulty occurred that came near overturning these peaceful relations and gaining for us their lasting enmity.

A military expedition consisting of four companies of the 1st Infantry and six companies of the 6th, commanded by General Atkinson, in that year ascended the Missouri for the purpose of treating with the various tribes and impressing them with the power of the United States. The greater part of the Crows chanced that year to make one of their customary visits of trade and amity to their kindred, the Minnetarees, and there met the troops, whom they viewed with interest and curiosity but without awe. They had with them a captive half-breed woman and child whom General Atkinson wished to liberate and, in the conference that ensued, Major O'Fallon became so much enraged at the taunts of a Crow chief that he snapped a pistol in his face and then struck him with the butt a violent blow on the head, inflicting a severe wound. The chief received the blow in sullen silence; but when the Indians outside the council tent heard of the occurrence, they became furious with rage and threatened an immediate attack upon the troops. In the confusion that ensued they succeeded in secretly spiking General Atkinson's cannon with sticks and stuffing them with earth and grass. But fortunately the affair was settled without bloodshed, mainly through the instrumentality of the renegade Rose, whom we have seen separate himself from a party of trappers at the Crow village eighteen years before. Peace being restored, the Crows of their own accord surrendered the half-breed woman and child, and General Atkinson rewarded them with a present of guns and ammunition.

After the abandonment of Lisa's fort at the mouth of Big Horn River, in 1808, the Crows were for many years without a trading post; but the roving bands of trappers and traders that after the year 1822 overspread the country kept them well supplied with the commodities of civilization. Toward the year 1830 the American Fur Company began to extend its trade up the Missouri River, and in 1829 built Fort Union near the mouth of the Yellowstone. The trade of the Crows was of too much consequence to be ignored, and within two years Fort Cass had been built within the limits of their country upon the Big Horn, to be replaced in 1835 by Fort Van Buren at the mouth of that stream. The Crows were anxious to retain a trading post in their country, but proved vacillating in choice of location, and at their request it was several times changed, the last establishment, Fort Sarpy, built in 1850, being located upon the Yellowstone a few miles below the mouth of Rosebud River. Five years later this post was abandoned, and was the last maintained by this company on the Yellowstone. The Company did not by this step lose the trade of the Crows, for the roving traders had passed away and thus, having no other resort, the tribe carried its peltries to the post at the mouth of the Yellowstone. Their annual sale amounted in those days to about five thousand robes. They were prudent purchasers, generally accepting nothing that did not serve them a useful purpose—as arms, ammunition, blankets, and beads. They would not drink whisky—differing therein from all the surrounding tribes—and it was therefore never kept at this post.

About the same time that the American Fur Company carried its trade up the Yellowstone to the Crows, it extended it higher up the Missouri to the Blackfeet bands. The Blackfeet were the inveterate, deadly enemies of the Crows, and, greatly outnumbering them, had the advantage in their wars. It displeased the Crows greatly to see a post maintained among their enemies that kept them abundantly supplied with civilized arms, and, finding remonstrances to fail in procuring its discontinuance, determined to reduce it by force. Therefore, in June, 1834, taking with them their lodges and families, they marched against it in heavy force, the fort being then garrisoned by Major Culbertson with twenty men. Pitching their camp about a quarter of a mile from its walls, they made themselves comfortable and prepared for a lengthened stay. It was not their desire to harm the garrison but only to starve it into surrender, when they intended to possess themselves of the goods, destroy the fort, and send its occupants out of the country. In pursuance of this plan the Indians kept them cooped up within its walls, but did not fire a shot.

The besieged dug a well in the fort, by which they had a plentiful supply of water; but their provisions soon began to fail. The fresh meat gave out in a day or two, then the dried meat reserved for an emergency was consumed, and finally the few dogs kept about the fort were killed and eaten. Still the grim warriors hung persistently about, and showed no disposition to depart. The only resource of the garrison was now pieces of raw buffalo hide and parfleches used to hold pounded meat. These were boiled until soft, when they presented an appearance similar to carpenter's glue. It was disgusting food—preserving life but wholly failing to satisfy the cravings of hunger. Hitherto the garrison had forborne to fire upon the Crows, though fair opportunities were daily presented. Knowing the fickleness of Indian character Major Culbertson had expected them ere long to tire of the investment and raise the siege, but, reduced to the last extremity, he now warned them to depart, threatening to fire upon them if they did not comply. They laughed at the menace and still remained. Then, on the tenth day of the siege, one of the cannon with which the fort was armed was charged with a solid shot, aimed at the center of the camp, and fired.

The effect was magical. It was a kind of war they were not accustomed to, and in a moment all was confusion. Lodges were down in a twinkling. There was a rapid gathering of horses, and in a few minutes the whole village was skurrying away at full speed up the river. The siege was raised. A few of the Crows crossed the river and opened fire upon the fort from the opposite bluffs, but did no harm. They soon left the vicinity, and thus ended the first, last, and only warlike attempt ever made by the Crows as a tribe upon the whites. The chief who led this attack was the Arapooash[23] so celebrated by Irving in his adventures of Bonneville. The English translation is Rotten Belly, a fact which Irving declined to disclose. He was killed soon afterward by the Blackfeet.

Another celebrated chief of those early days was Long Hair, between whom and Arapooash a rivalry existed that divided the nation. As had occurred fifty years before, the tribe sep-

23 Irving spells this name with an "i"—Arapooish.

arated into two camps, rather less than one-third following Arapooash while the remainder acknowledged the leadership of Long Hair. Though frequently uniting their forces, they were generally asunder and began to haunt different localities, the followers of Long Hair remaining generally south of the Yellowstone on Clark's Fork and the Big Horn, while the band of Arapooash frequented the valley of the Judith and Mussel-shell and sometimes ranged to the Missouri. The separation at last became so complete that the whites gave to the bands different names, distinguishing them according to their different haunts as Mountain and River Crows—names they still bear. They are on terms of friendship, exchange visits, and occasionally unite their camps; but differences of habit are growing up that will probably prevent their ever coalescing again, though some of the older men, who knew the tribe as one, yet cherish dreams of reunion.

When, in 1834, the trading post of Fort Laramie was built near the mouth of the river of that name, an invitation was extended to the Sioux to move over into its neighborhood. The invitation was accepted by about one hundred lodges of Ogallallas under Bull Bear, who ere long began to encroach upon the southern borders of the country of the Crows. The latter were soon driven from the North Platte, and afterward confined their range to the northward of Powder River. About twenty years later other bands of the Sioux, finding the buffalo diminishing in their own country, began to press to the westward and soon came into contact with the Crows in the excursions of the latter to the mouth of the Yellowstone.

The expulsion of the Santee Sioux from Minnesota after the massacre in that state gave new impulse to this movement, and the Crows, unable to resist so formidable an invasion, withdrew more and more to the north and west until at last the Sioux were in full possession of the lower Yellowstone, and the valleys of Powder, Tongue, Rosebud, and Big Horn rivers. Occasionally still the Crows venture in large camps to the latter stream, but only to retire hastily upon the approach of the dreaded Sioux. They may now be said to be confined to the left bank of Pryor's Creek, but even here they are incessantly harassed by the Sioux, and frequently filled by their approach with the wildest consternation. Their present entire strength is less than four hundred lodges, or only about one-fourth of that with which they migrated from the Kansas River 125 years ago.

They call themselves by the name of Up-sah-ro-ku (usually but incorrectly written Absaraka), a word whose meaning is lost.[24] The name of Crows, by which they are known to the whites, is a translation of the name long since applied to them by some of the surrounding tribes. They are firm friends of the whites, recognizing it as their best policy, and with judicious management upon the part of our Government will ever remain so. There are not wanting instances of the maltreating and killing of whites by members of the tribe, but they are comparatively rare, confined to the worst element of the tribe, and disapproved of by the general sentiment. In a remarkable tradition of the creation possessed by them, it is said that, as men increased in number upon the face of the earth, the spirits who had created them divided them into tribes, though all as yet spoke one tongue. At length, however, the spirits called from above the earth bidding all to assemble themselves together; and when they had done so, the spirits gave to each tribe a different tongue, and none understood the tongue given to the others. The spirits also appointed to each tribe a certain place for a home, and then commanded all to shake hands together. There were people of all colors there,

---

[24] "Home of the Crows"; See *AB-SA-RA-KA, the Land of Massacre*, by Col. Henry B. Carrington.—W. E. S.

but the white people stood nearest to the spirits, and, after they had shaken hands, the spirits said so as to be heard by all: "All people are dear to us, but the white people are dearest of all; we command you always to live at peace with the white people." Then the assembly dispersed, and the tribes spread themselves over all the land. And surely this injunction of what they take to be divine authority has been better obeyed by the Crows than are behests from the same high source by their brethren of the white-skin.

Monday, May 1. About noon four of the Crows, who had crossed the river and gone up to the mouth of the Big Horn, were seen running rapidly along the summit of the rocky ridge on the opposite shore, occasionally describing the circle that indicates an enemy seen. When they got near enough to be heard, they shouted that the Sioux were close at hand and begged that a boat be sent over for them instantly. The boat was sent, and they were soon safe on this side telling their story, which was to the effect that dense swarms of mounted men in three bodies were pouring down Tullock's Fork, that they were undoubtedly Sioux, and that we might expect them soon to attack the camp. This information caused no excitement, as Capt. Ball was expected to return today, and by way of Tullock's Fork, so that the mounted men were pretty certain to prove to be his two companies of cavalry. And so it turned out, for about 3 P.M. he arrived in camp. He had ascended the Big Horn to old Fort C. F. Smith, crossed over to the Little Big Horn, thence passed to the upper part of Tullock's Fork and descended this stream to its junction with the Big Horn, without having encountered the Sioux or seen any recent sign of them. The officers speak in the highest terms of the beauty and fertility of some of the country they traversed on the trip. The ruins of Fort C. F. Smith are still in a good state of preservation, though the place was abandoned eight years ago. Its adobe walls do not yield to the incendiary's torch, or the Sioux would have long since got rid of them.

We are now minus six of our Crows—three who deserted the other day, and the three who left us at Pompey's Pillar on the seventeenth ultimo to accompany the party of Crow volunteers on their scout. We hear that this party scouted to the Rosebud and then returned to the Crow camp, our three scouts going with them instead of rejoining us with the information gained, as they had been ordered to. This evening Bravo, interpreter, and one of the Crows, Little Face, were sent back to the agency, bearing a letter to the agent, who is requested to use his influence to get these six renegades to return. Bravo has much ill-merited influence over the Crows and Little Face is a good old fellow who will do all he can, and the chances are we will get them all back. Little Face's son is among the absentees. They are allowed eleven days for the round trip.

Tuesday, 2. An uneventful day in camp. A good deal of speculation is rife in the command as to the whereabouts of the Sioux. We have now been two weeks in their country, a protracted scout has been made by the cavalry up the Big Horn and another by the Crows down to Rosebud River, and all without discovering a vestige of them. It is not long since Crook routed them on Powder River, so they are not likely to be lingering there. Where are they? The question is answered in different ways, but the general impression seems to be that having learned, as they undoubtedly have, the extensive preparations making for waging war upon them, they have become frightened and resorted to the agencies, where under the protecting aegis of the Indian Bureau they have been transformed from implacable, blood-thirsty war-

L. A. Huffman photograph

POMPEY'S PILLAR

Northern Pacific Railway

GENERAL CUSTER IN MONTANA TERRITORY IN THE 1870's.

riors into good, peaceable Indians, and where they will stay fattening on government rations, accumulating the means of waging renewed war, but crying, Peace! Peace! until the storm blows over, when they will again take the field and resume their old trade of shedding whitemen's blood.

Wednesday, 3. We have found the Sioux, or rather, they have found us. Reveille passed off as usual this morning, everyone turning out of bed and falling into ranks to answer to his name, and then turning into bed and falling asleep for another doze. But presently it was discovered that Bostwick's horse (Shavy) and mule, which had been picketed out the evening before to graze just outside the line of sentinels and about three hundred yards from camp, were gone. Investigation proved them to have been taken by Sioux, and as soon as the Crows heard of the circumstance, they rushed to the island just above camp where they had left their horses over night to graze, but every head was gone—thirty-two in all, gobbled by the Sioux. A search around the camp disclosed the fact that they had been in close vicinity to our sentinels, a broken saddle, three blankets, several wiping-sticks and other articles being found. The rascals managed the thing very adroitly, indeed.

The Crows had a good cry over their loss, standing together in a row and shedding copious tears, after which they set out to follow the trail of the robbers. It was found to lead down the valley to a point about eight miles below, where it crossed the stream. The Crows heard shots upon the opposite bank, which seemed to indicate that the Sioux were not very anxious to get out of the way and had little dread of pursuit. Fearing to cross, the Crows turned back. The trail indicates that about fifty Sioux were engaged in the affair, about twenty of whom reconnoitered our camp and secured the horses while the remainder held themselves in reserve a little way off. Of the seventeen Crows now with us, not one has a horse. It is an unfortunate state of affairs, as it will greatly impair their usefulness as scouts. The General has been disposed to allow them every possible latitude to prevent the restraints of service from becoming too irksome to them, and so has permitted them to look after their horses in their own way, believing that their instinct and training would enable them to judge rightly what precautions were necessary. As commander of the scouts, and therefore personally concerned, I will add this has not been my theory. I have desired to practice a more rigorous discipline with the Crows, and would have done so had I been unrestrained.

In the afternoon there was an alarm that the Sioux had got the herd, which was grazing about a mile up the valley. A light snow had been falling and a heavy fog overhung the valley, concealing distant objects, out of which two or three animals could be seen galloping towards camp. We were quickly under arms, but it proved to be a false alarm.

Groff and Madden, of my detachment, went out hunting this morning before we learned of the presence of the Sioux. Groff has returned but can give no account of Madden, who is still absent. With the Sioux around, his position is critical.

Thursday, 4. During last night two couriers arrived bringing mail. They had been fired upon after dark about ten miles from camp, but were not pursued. Sergt. Farrell with five men of my detachment, LeForgey, and one Crow, went out at 7 A.M. to look for Madden, returning with him at 3 P.M. It is a great relief to find him alive, but he has had a narrow escape. When found he was traveling directly away from camp, being completely bewildered. He had passed the night under an overhanging rock which sheltered him from the snow, but he had no food. It was found that a Sioux trail crossed his. This was probably made by the party who had fired on the couriers; and they must have crossed during the night, as had they seen it, they would undoubtedly have followed and killed him. As bewildered men are so apt to do, he traveled in a circle, and after going several miles this morning found himself back at the rock where he had passed the night.

The General had a conference with the Crows today and tried to induce them to go in search of a Sioux camp, but they declined, saying the time had passed by when the Indians could go to war on foot, their enemies being too well mounted.

Friday, 5. Sent the Crows all out on foot today to follow back the trail of the Sioux as we are anxious to learn if possible where they are from—whether from down the river or across the country from Fort Peck. In due time they returned with the information that the trail keeps the north bank of the Yellowstone, heading from below and apparently from the interior, but they feared to follow it on foot far enough to settle the point. Requested and obtained the General's permission to mount two Crows on my own horses and send them tomorrow several miles farther out on the trail to try and obtain additional information.

Saturday, 6. Mounted Half Yellow Face on my own horse (Mink) this morning, and gave Jack Rabbit Bull a good mount also, and started them off on the Sioux trail. They followed it some fifteen miles, finding that the Sioux thieves had not come from the interior, as had been surmised, but from some point on the river below us. As they were cautiously advancing, they discovered three Sioux near the river about a mile in their front, and, waiting until their enemies had disappeared from view behind a ridge, charged them boldly at full speed. They were close on the Sioux before the latter discovered their approach, and, ignorant of the numbers assailing them, the Sioux fled into the broken ground near the river, abandoning three horses to the Crows. These were quickly secured and the triumphant Crows beat a hasty retreat to our camp, where they arrived early in the afternoon, proud of their exploit and three horses richer for it. It was a daring deed, for the three Sioux they saw might have been merely lookouts of a heavy force near at hand.

It is very unlikely that this small party of Sioux are alone, and I requested the General's permission to take my detachment and some of the Crows and make a night march down the river to see what I could find. He at first refused, but finally consented, though he postponed the departure till tomorrow night. I had wished to start this evening, fearing the Sioux, if in small force, may leave tonight.

Sunday, 7. Captain Clifford says in his journal of this date: "The entire force of scouts went down the river and are very liable to be scooped up by an overwhelming force of Sioux." This alludes to the departure of my detachment on the scout arranged yesterday, and expresses the general feeling of the camp over our enterprise. The General evidently felt great misgivings, and I feared he would revoke the permission to go, but he did not. Myself and men passed the day in preparation, and as soon as it was dark enough to conceal our departure, we mounted and rode forth, the greater part of the command gathering to see us off, many looking on us as doomed men. The detachment consisted of seventeen soldiers, citizen Bostwick, LeForgey, and four Crows—twenty-five including myself.

We marched continuously down the valley and found fresh pony tracks six miles out, showing that the Sioux are hovering around us. Made careful disposition of the command with reference to a possible ambuscade and moved on, but the darkness of the night and the necessity of great caution in passing through the thickets in the valley made our progress annoyingly slow. Ten miles down the valley ran out against the river bluffs, which we ascended, and for five miles crossed the highlands at fair speed. We were now near the scene of yesterday's exploit, and advanced with great care. Presently the low wolf cry, that signals the enemy, came from the scouts in front. It was an excellent imitation and would have deceived anyone. They had found some moccasins, and a little farther on distinguished three war lodges through the gloom —shelter for about thirty men. That was the number I wanted to strike, but alas! for our hopes of performing an exploit, they were gone. They had left a hatchet and some other trifling articles, and appeared to have been gone about twenty-four hours. Had they still been there, we would probably have destroyed the most of them, for they rarely keep out sentinels in such expeditions, and we could have been upon them ere they were aware of our presence. These lodges are about a mile from the place where the two Crows captured the three horses, and so it turned out that the Sioux they saw were but three of thirty and that the two bold Crows were in great peril indeed.

Monday, 8. It was about 3 A.M. when we struck the three war lodges. Thinking the Sioux might have moved down the river a few miles and camped again, I determined to pass on. The remainder of our night's ride led down the left bank of the stream, through a succession of thickets and openings, and across the tributary of the Yellowstone called by the Crows "They-froze-to-death," some of their tribe having once perished there in that manner. The whites call it, in doubtful English, Froze-to-death Creek. Just as it was getting light we found more Sioux sign, where a party of them had crossed the river to the opposite bank. Desiring to take an observation before advancing farther, we turned off to a high point favorable for the purpose, about two miles from the river, within whose clefts and depressions we could conceal our horses and see without being seen. Here we unsaddled and fed the horses while the Crows looked out for smoke or other indications of a camp, but made no discoveries. Thousands of buffalo were grazing quietly in the valley and on the hills.

Satisfied that there was no party or camp within striking distance I saddled up after a few hours' stay and moved down into the valley, where again we found Sioux sign. Among the other tracks Bostwick recognized that of his lost mule, which he knew by the shoe marks. The tracks were about two days old, and kept down the left bank of the Yellowstone. Judging by the trails and other indications I should say that, after capturing the Crow ponies, the Sioux divided, about twenty pressing on rapidly with their plunder while the remainder, about thirty in number, remained behind to watch our movements, but have now, since their discovery by the Crows, gone off also. We continued down the valley for three or four miles, and finding a good place to graze, halted, posted lookouts, unsaddled, and rested from 10:30 A.M. to 5 P.M.

Here we found more Sioux sign—war lodges, horse and moccasin tracks, fresh ashes, and an elaborate arrangement of buffalo-chips and skulls for "making medicine." It was probably a stopping place of the Sioux on their way up to our camp, the sign appearing just about old enough. Resuming the march at 5 P.M., we passed down the valley about two miles to the Great Porcupine Creek, where we found a large band of buffalo, and before I knew what their intentions were, the Crows were chasing them at full speed firing into the herd. They killed several and the meat was acceptable enough, but the firing might have brought the Sioux down upon us. The carelessness of these fellows at times is simply amazing. One would think that the Indian's life of constant exposure to danger would make caution and precaution so much his habit that he would never lay them aside, but it is quite otherwise. In my scouts with the Crows I was compelled to watch them constantly to prevent the doing of some foolish or foolhardy thing that might have betrayed us to an enemy and brought destruction on us all.

As there was nothing to be gained by a farther advance, we turned up the valley of the Great Porcupine, homeward bound, followed it six miles, ascended one of its tributaries— a dry ravine—till it ran out in the prairie, and then crossed to Froze-to-death Creek, where we camped at 2 A.M.

Tuesday, 9. Saddled up and marched at 8 A.M., crossed the prairie for a distance of about twelve miles, struck the Yellowstone valley about six miles below camp, which we reached about noon, having seen no Sioux sign during the return trip. In the course of this scout we traveled about eighty-five miles.

Captains Freeman and Logan had arrived yesterday. After leaving our camp on the twenty-third ult., Captain Freeman marched up the left bank of the Yellowstone, arriving at Captain Logan's camp above Clark's Fork at 9 A.M. on the twenty-eighth. The train was loaded the following day, and on the thirtieth both companies began their march to Fort Pease, Lieutenant Kendrick with an escort of ten men of Co. H, 7th Infantry, continuing on to Fort Ellis with the discharged contract wagons of Power's train.

At last after twenty days' delay we are under orders to move down the river to co-operate with the force that is about to leave Fort Abraham Lincoln under Custer. We march in the morning. Upon our arrival at Fort Pease we found several boats which had been abandoned by the garrison, the best of which have been put in repair and are to be taken with us. Captain Clifford's Company E has been assigned to the duty of navigating them, and I am ordered to furnish him with two Indians to do the necessary scouting along shore. Two couriers left this evening bearing mail.

Wednesday, 10. Marched at 8:45 A. M., my detachment in advance, Captain Clifford's company in the boats. Marched seventeen miles, the last few through a drenching rain, and camped in the valley at 7:30 P. M. The train had a hard pull out of the valley; the latter half of the march was across the table-land. A mail arrived today. The Crows picked up a couple of poor horses—evidently lost or abandoned by Sioux.

Thursday, May 11. It was ascertained this morning that the Sioux are hanging around us again. The Crows found a place in the willows close to camp where four of them had lain last night. We remained in camp today.

Friday, 12. Marched at 7 A. M., following Stanley's trail of 1873,[25] and camped in the Yellowstone Valley at 5:30 P. M., having marched nineteen miles. Our last camp was just below the point where I found the three war lodges on the night of the seventh; the present one is about three hundred yards from my nooning place of the eighth. The thousands of buffalo then in this vicinity are gone. Captain Clifford found some fresh Sioux sign along the banks of the river today. Toward evening Bravo and Little Face returned from their trip to the agency and brought back with them the six Crow deserters. They have done well. This gives us eight more mounted scouts—ten in all.

Saturday, 13. We passed the day in camp. Lieutenant Jacobs with Taylor, Bostwick, and Sergeant Wilson (who accompanied me on the seventh), crossed the river and scouted

25 In 1873, General David S. Stanley had commanded an expedition escorting the surveyors for the route of the Northern Pacific Railroad. They had gone as far west at Pompey's Pillar. Custer, with the Seventh Cavalry, was a part of this force and had had several brushes with the Sioux.—E. I. S.

toward the Rosebud, intending to have gone to that stream, but, mistaking a small creek therefor, turned back without reaching it. They found no Sioux sign. Four of the Crows crossed the river in the evening, and have gone off on foot to look for a Sioux camp. They all carried lariats, and their object is to steal horses to provide themselves with a remount. I heartily wish they may be successful, for they are of little use to us on foot.

Two of the Crows got into a quarrel this morning over the ownership of one of the Sioux horses found on the tenth inst., and at last one of them in a rage drew his knife and settled the dispute by killing the horse. Instead of resenting the act, the other, when he saw what his adversary was about to do, whipped out his knife also and assisted in the killing, a few amicable stabs upon the part of each in the poor beast's body sufficing to restore good feeling between them.

Sunday, 14. Marched at 8 A.M., reached Great Porcupine Creek in two miles, and had considerable difficulty in crossing it. During the delay thus created I visited a notable rock which towers over the Yellowstone valley a couple of miles from the junction of the two streams. It has generally been called Castle Rock. The rock rises perpendicularly out of a conical clay peak, the whole towering between two and three hundred feet above the valley. Being desirous of the view, I made strenuous efforts to climb it, and at great risk to neck and limb finally attained the summit and left my name and the date inscribed thereon. The summit bore signs of Indian visitors, and it is said to be a favorite lookout for Sioux and Crows.

Marched seventeen miles, and camped at 4:30 P.M. in the Yellowstone valley. The road lay mainly down the valley, but once ascended to the high grounds and returned to the valley through a long, devious, deep ravine, affording unlimited facilities for an ambuscade. Soon after camp was formed, a terrific hail storm suddenly burst upon us, accompanied by a high wind and followed by a deluge of rain. The herd stampeded to the camp and into the timber, tents were blown down, pools formed all through the camp, drowning out the occupants of many tents which stood in some cases in nearly a foot of water, everybody got wet, and a good many lost their suppers.

Major Brisbin and Lieutenants English and Johnson were among the unfortunates that the wind left out of doors. It was a terrible storm, but soon subsided; and there was a busy time through the rest of the afternoon moving and repitching tents, fishing personal effects out of the water and mud, and reclaiming the stampeded animals. It continued to rain most of the night, the tents all leaked, bedding was drenched, and we had rather a cheerless time of it. This camp will long linger in the memory of its unfortunate occupants as Hail-stone or Drowned-out camp.

Monday, 15. We lay in camp today, the road being too muddy to admit of marching. A scouting party of Crows went down the river a few miles, but returned without having found any Sioux sign. The war party that left our camp on the thirteenth inst., returned today about 10 o'clock A.M. Yesterday they struck a trail indicating about thirty mounted Sioux leading up the river on the opposite side, and followed it in the hope of catching the party in camp in the evening and getting off with their horses. But the storm came on, completely obliterating the trail, the night was intensely dark, and unable to accomplish anything, they gave up the pursuit and returned disheartened to camp.

After gathering the story of the Crows, I reported with it to the General, and then requested permission to do a little village-hunting myself, stating my belief that the thirty Sioux whose trail had been found by the Crows had come from a village on Tongue River, and promising to find it if there was one there. After some hesitation, fearing the destruction of my detachment, he finally consented, leaving the details to me. I made up a party consisting of twelve men of my detachment, eight volunteers from the infantry companies, and Bravo with five Crows—twenty-seven including myself. I had hoped for some volunteers from the cavalry, having been promised some by Major Brisbin, but none came forward. During the day three days' rations were got ready and other preparations made, and toward evening the men left camp one by one so as not to excite suspicion of a watchful enemy, and gathered upon the bank of the river covered by the timber. The river was very high and running like a mill-race, but aided by Captain Clifford with his boats we crossed in about twenty minutes without accident, swimming the horses, and just at dark all were assembled upon the opposite bank. The most of the command had gathered to see us off, and a good deal of apprehension was felt on our behalf, not a few feeling assured that we would never return.

Covered by the darkness we began our march, climbing the river bluffs and crossing the high ground toward the Rosebud. The route pursued was terrible—up hill and down, through muddy gullies, and along steep, slippery hillsides, tiring out men and horses and wasting precious time. The Crows had said openly that we were going to certain destruction, and it had been hard to get out of the whole band the requisite number for the scout, none volunteering, so that I had been obliged to make a detail of the five I took. Being aware of their reluctance and timidity I became convinced that they were purposely selecting a bad route to tire me out, waste time, and induce me to abandon the undertaking; and finally I halted the column and gave them a severe lecture. I was satisfied from their replies that I had not misjudged them, and assured them that we would go to Tongue River if it took a month, threatening to become my own guide if they did not do better, when we might run into dangers that we could avoid if they did as well as they might. Seeing they had nothing to gain by their subterfuge, they agreed to do the best they could, and pushing on we soon emerged into a better country. We passed the Rosebud some five miles out, and, traveling about nine miles farther, halted soon after midnight in a grassy ravine which the Crows assured me was near the base of the Wolf Mountains. As it was not safe to pass these hills without first taking a view of the surrounding country, I unsaddled, posted a guard, and let the men sleep and the horses graze till daylight.

May: Tuesday, 16. Found this morning, when it grew light, that the Crows had deceived me and that we were yet about five miles from the Wolf Mountains. Saddled up at 4 o'clock and moved on, reaching the hills about 6. The morning was slightly foggy, which conduced to our safety, but about the time we reached the hills it cleared off, leaving the day beautifully bright. Finding a sheltered cove where the grass was good and concealment perfect, I unsaddled and went with the Crows to the top of a promising peak, from which an excellent view was obtained. We had a fair view of the Rosebud from its mouth upward for over thirty miles, within which there was no smoke or other sign of a camp, nor was there any anywhere within our range of view. A ridge of considerable elevation interposed between us and Tongue River, so that we could not tell what might be there.

Spent about three hours in making these observations, then saddled up and moved on. We soon struck the trail of the thirty Sioux who passed up the river a day or two ago, and became satisfied it led from Tongue River at a point some fifteen or eighteen miles above its mouth. We were now pretty sure of finding a village, and it became necessary to travel with the utmost caution, keeping concealed as much as possible. We effected this by marching in ravines wherever they offered, under cover of the knolls that were occasionally presented, and finally by ascending the summit of a wooded ridge, whose pine timber screened us completely for several miles. When necessary to pass over open ground we closed up in a solid mass and dashed across it as quickly as possible. Two of the Crows, mounted on gray horses (which show least from a distance), were kept two or three hundred yards in advance, and when we reached especially open ground they were sent to the summit of the next ridge in front before the main body showed itself. With all these precautions it would have required a very watchful enemy indeed to discover our advance.

About 4 o'clock in the afternoon the two Crows in front signaled that they had made a discovery. They were then on the summit of a ridge, and, placing the detachment in a basin-like depression near by where it was hidden from view on all sides but one, I joined them and found that our village was at hand. Tongue River lay between five and six miles in our front, the timber showing through one break in the bluffs, while up and down the stream the smoke was rising in different columns and uniting in a cloud which hung low over the valley. Nothing could be more certain than that it marked the presence of an Indian village, though we could not see a single teepee on account of the interposing bluffs. While we lay watching it, hundreds of buffalo which had been quietly feeding between us and the river became suddenly agitated, and the whole in bands of from ten to a hundred fled at full speed across our front to the right. Herd after herd that we had not seen before came into view over the hills on our left, some passing in our front, others in our rear, until I estimated that not less than five thousand had gone by. One of these bands, about twenty in number, came directly toward us, the wind not betraying our presence, and only swerved from their course when they reached the summit of the ridge and were within twenty yards of us.

For a time this stampede of the buffalo filled us with apprehension lest we had been discovered by the Sioux, whose sallying forth to meet us had occasioned it; but the Crows soon became satisfied it arose from the movements of the Sioux hunters lower down the stream, and their reasons appeared satisfactory. There was danger, however, that the hunters might continue their pursuit into our neighborhood; once we thought we detected a couple of mounted men skurrying over a ridge a couple of miles distant, but they did not reappear, and we might have been mistaken.

Becoming satisfied that we had not yet been discovered, I formed the plan of remaining where we were until dark, approaching then with the detachment as near as the conformation of the ground might render prudent, and going on myself with Bravo and one or two of the Indians, all on foot, sufficiently near to see the lodges and get an idea of their number. This scheme, however, the Crows with one accord violently opposed, arguing that it would be sure to result in our discovery and destruction; and it was evident that they sincerely believed that no white man had the address necessary to the successful management of such an enterprise. I would not let them go alone, as nothing was more certain than that their horse-stealing proclivities would get the better of them so that, in their effort to possess themselves of a few Sioux ponies, they would be liable to bring the whole village down upon us. But they were not anxious to undertake it, and insisted that our best course was to get back as fast as possible. No Indian, they said would think of asking better evidence of a village than we already had in the peculiar smoke which could only come from a number of such small fires as are built in Indian camps. To want actually to see the lodges they laughed at as a ridiculous idea, for even in respect to the number they could estimate sufficiently near from the smoke; and in this case they were satisfied that there were not less than two or three hundred.

Finding that I could not rely upon them to assist me in the execution of my night enterprise, I resolved to accept their advice and return. It had been the hope of my men that we would encounter a party or find a camp sufficiently weak for us to attack, and when they had learned that a village was before us, they awaited impatiently my decision respecting it. When, therefore, I returned and calling them around me informed them that unfortunately for our hopes of a conquest we had struck a village of several hundred lodges, and that our only chance of life depended on getting away from it without being discovered, there were more that looked disappointed than showed anxiety. It afterward turned out that this camp contained about four hundred lodges, or from eight hundred to a thousand warriors, but for all that there were not wanting men among those bold rascals of mine that would have had me attack it with our twenty-seven. But they all lived to be thankful that we didn't. A sight of the Custer field, six weeks later, with its 206 naked and bloody corpses, the victims in part of this very village, satisfied them that we had done well not to poke a stick into the hive.

At 6 o'clock we mounted and set out on our return, having been in the vicinity of the camp for two hours. We traveled briskly for about an hour when, finding water, I halted, fed the animals the last of the grain we had brought, allowed the men to eat their supper, and then moved on. Being at a safe distance from the village and knowing that the country was clear, we traveled with less regard to concealment, leaving to the right the difficult wooded heights we had been so glad of in the forenoon, and making good time. Continued the march till half-past nine, then halted, unsaddled, and rested two hours, allowing the men to sleep, and again pushed on. The night was very dark, but now that we were going in the direction of their desires, the Crows showed an excellent knowledge of the country, and led us by an easy route. Knowing that we had somewhere in our front the thirty Sioux who passed up the river, we kept the best possible lookout and traveled silently.

Wednesday, 17. Traveled all night, crossed the Rosebud just at daybreak (a little higher up than our first crossing), and about half an hour after sunrise arrived upon the bluffs overlooking the camp. I had feared the command might have moved, and was glad to find it still where we left it. A boat was soon sent over to me, and leaving my detachment on the margin of the stream, I crossed and made my report to the General. The command was under orders to march and was then packing up preparatory to so doing; but, after an hour's deliberation, the General countermanded the order and issued another to get ready at once to cross the river for the purpose of moving on the Sioux village.

It was two months to a day since we had left Fort Shaw for the purpose of cleaning out the Sioux nation, and during all that time we had done nothing but march, march, and rest in camp; but now the enemy had been found and we were going over to whip them. The accumulated satisfaction of the sixty blessed days that had preceded, if combined in a single lump, could not have equaled that with which this order was received. Not that there were no soreheads who were personified gloom and despondency and whispered of dire overthrow and dreadful disaster; but the great majority were hopeful, jubilant, and full of the fire of battle. Everybody fell to with a will, and there was more real good feeling and enthusiasm in the camp than I had witnessed in a body of men for a long time. But there came a sober, serious time to most of us, and that was when we sat down to pen to the far-off loved ones letters that might be the last they would ever receive from us. We did not then credit the Sioux with the prowess we have since learned to, but still we did not despise our foe, and felt that the fight would probably be well enough contested to make some vacancies among us.

Among the most enthusiastic were the Crows, who had chafed under the disgrace they had suffered in the abstraction of their horses and who now beamed with satisfaction at the prospect presented of recovering from their hated enemies their own with usury. They announced their determination to fight, and I have no doubt that to a degree they would have done so and some of them very bravely; but I feel sure that within the tawny hides of the greater number lurked the resolution to leave the bulk of the fighting to the *mahrstaksheedah* —as they call us—and devote their choicest energies to the gathering in of the stray ponies of the Sioux.

Captain Sanno's company (K) of the infantry was to remain in charge of the camp, the rest of the force constituting the column to advance against the Sioux. This column comprised five companies of infantry and four of cavalry, the mounted detachment, and Crow scouts, numbering in the aggregate 34 officers and 350 men, including the Crow scouts, to which are to be added about eight of our civilian camp followers, making our total effective force 392 men. We were to carry one blanket and 150 rounds of ammunition per man, and seven days' rations, thirty pack mules being provided as transportation. Taking as a basis the time occupied by my detachment in crossing, it was estimated that the entire command would be over by dark, when we would have made a forced march and got as near the village as possible before daylight, being governed by circumstances as to the time and method of attack.

To render the camp as compact and defensible as possible, the most of the tents were taken down, and Captain Sanno bestirred himself vigorously in the construction of rifle-pits and other preparations for defense. The cavalry were ordered to cross first, the infantry holding themselves in readiness to follow as soon as the cavalry were done with the boats. The crossing began about noon, perhaps a little earlier, at a point about a mile above the camp, and for four mortal hours it went on at a most tedious, discouraging rate, about ten animals being got over per hour, though the officers and men engaged in it seemed to have done their best. What the trouble was I did not then understand, and I don't now, and I have never seen anybody that did. Everything worked at cross purposes, accident succeeded accident, and at last, after many narrow escapes on the part of both men and horses, four of the latter were drowned. The General had evidently chafed under the delay, but, where to all appearances everything was being done that men could do, saw no chance to accelerate matters. It had become evident that not even the cavalry would be over by dark, and when there came the catastrophe of the drowning of the four horses, it proved to be the last straw that broke the back of our warlike enterprise. Orders were given to recross the cavalry horses already over the river and my detachment, which had remained on the other side, and the expedition was abandoned. Before dark we were all together again in camp, tents were repitched, and everything had settled into its accustomed state.

And so we failed to march against the foe. There ever will

be a difference of opinion as to the propriety of the course pursued, but as I am not writing a critical history I will not take this advantage of my fellow officers to record mine. . . .[26]

The Crows who, when the order to advance on the village was given, were the most jubilant, were now, on the other hand, the most crestfallen and depressed. The crossing of a stream is such a simple matter for them that they do not understand how it should have proved an insuperable obstacle to our advance, and they are inclined to look upon it as a device to conceal our cowardice. I often talk with them and explain the mysteries and advantages of our prolonged movements and combined operations of different columns, which appear very perplexing compared to their simple methods of a dash in and out with a single force, but I fear it all avails little when they recall to mind a little passage that occurred in the course of our council with them in April. Said one of their speakers, Old Crow: "If the Crows go with you, and they find a camp, they will bark like a dog. Will you then jump on the camp and fight right there?"

General Gibbon—"That is what we want."

Old Crow—"That is good."

One circumstance remains to be mentioned that had undoubtedly much to do with the General's decision not to march on the camp. Within an hour after my arrival from the village, the Sioux appeared in view on the prairie on the opposite side of the stream. My first impression was that it was the party of thirty returning from their bootless up-river trip; but those who saw the Indians estimated their number at not less than seventy-five, so that it must have been a party from the village on Tongue River. They had undoubtedly become in some way aware of our visit and followed us in; and had not the darkness favored us, we should probably

[26] Ellipsis indicated in original publication of the Journal.—E. I. S.

have had to fight before we got back. They remained in the vicinity all day, killed several buffalo in plain view of my men, and two or three times tried to creep upon them. In the afternoon, when I went over to recross my detachment, and sent the most of them over, they came down within two hundred yards of us. My guard gave the alarm, and seizing our guns, we charged up the hill, but by the time we gained the summit, they were far out of range. I counted seventeen still in sight, but there were undoubtedly men who were concealed from view by a swell of the prairie. Whether or not they knew we were trying to cross is uncertain, but it is fair to presume that they did. If so, it would of course have been impossible for us to surprise their camp.

During my absence from the camp only one incident occurred there that requires mention—a false alarm about 10 o'clock on the night of the sixteenth. The guard posted on the bank of the river over the boats imagined they saw in their front moving objects bearing a light, and taking them for Indians signaling, fired three shots at them, soon followed by two more. The command turned out, but upon investigation was dismissed. This fright of the guard occasioned the following terse criticism by one of our men, an old warrior of thirty odd years' service in the army: "Well, by God, I've lived a good many years, and seen lots of Indians, and served a good deal in their country, but these are the first Indians I ever knew to go hunting a camp of soldiers with a lantern."

A similar alarm occurred this evening at the same place. Three of my horses were missing, and, thinking that the guard might fire on them as they grazed toward the camp, I asked permission to take my detachment and go after them lest they be shot before morning. The guard pointed out to me the place where they had seen the moving objects, when I deployed the detachment and with arms in readiness moved in that direction. About three hundred yards from camp we came suddenly upon a small light, and without waiting for orders some of the men began to fire at it and had fired several shots before I could stop them. We then moved up to the light and found it to proceed from a nearly consumed log, there being just enough fire left to flash up like a torch when fanned by a gust of wind. We scouted around for about half an hour without finding the horses, but later in the night they approached the camp and were secured.

Thursday, 18. Road still bad and a rainy day, so that the command remained in camp. About noon Thompson's and Wheelan's companies of the cavalry left with three days' rations, accompanied by two Crows, to scout down to the mouth of Tongue River. The object is presumed to be to discover promptly any disposition upon the part of the Sioux to leave the south side of the river, where it is desirable that they be kept until the forces converging upon them arrive within co-operating distance of each other. If they can be confined to the south bank, some one of our columns will be pretty sure to strike them, whereas, if they escape into the vast, difficult country to the north, they could more easily elude pursuit, if necessary crossing the line into the British Possessions.

In the afternoon four of the Crows crossed the river with the design of proceeding on foot to the Sioux village to steal horses.

Soon after the cavalry companies left, the General ordered me to march at dark with my detachment on a three days' scout up the river, or until we meet a party of couriers now due. I started as soon as it was dark enough to leave unobserved, taking twelve of my detachment, Le Forgey, and five Crows, traveled twelve miles and halted to rest and graze, bivouacking without fire at the foot of the river bluffs. Twice during the night the horses became restless, rearing and snorting with alarm; and once the sentinel reported a moving object in the valley. Took LeForgey and one Indian and scouted around the camp, but could discover nothing, and concluded that there were buffalo about. A heavy dew fell, and being without bedding, we were chilled to the marrow of our bones.

Friday, 19. Daylight revealed an old buffalo bull grazing quietly some distance from our resting place, who was probably the innocent cause of our night's alarm. Saddled up and moved on just after sunrise. Striking a small band of buffalo just before reaching the Great Porcupine I gave the Crows permission to kill one, which they effected after a lively run, dropping him in an excellent place for a halt. Stopped therefore to enable the men to butcher him and get breakfast. Having no fears that there were any considerable number of Sioux in the neighborhood, we built fires, made coffee and had a "square meal." While this was going on, I discovered, with the aid of my glass, two men on the bluffs about five miles up the river, who turned out to be the couriers we were looking for, arriving at our camp at about 9 o'clock. They had made a quick trip and seen no sign of Sioux; but had they happened along a couple of days earlier, they would probably have fallen into the hands of the thirty who passed up on the fourteenth. Again I repeat, this is a dangerous service.

As my orders were to return upon meeting the couriers, I remained only long enough to give them a breakfast and feed the animals grain, and about 10 o'clock took the back track. The day was quite showery. Stopped half an hour to lunch at a splendid mineral (sulphur and iron) spring situated at the point where the road leaves the valley; a real gem of a fountain pouring out a considerable stream of clear cold water. Reached camp at half-past three, bringing joy to the command, for the couriers bore an ample mail. We learn that

General Terry has taken the field in person, and that we may look for the arrival of Custer at the head of the entire 7th Cavalry in about a month. In the meantime we are ordered to remain in this vicinity and hold the Indians, if possible, on the south bank. At least two steamboats have been secured for service on the Yellowstone in connection with the movement of the troops—the "Josephine" and "Far West." There is plenty of water, and we are liable any day to see the black chimneys creeping around the headlands below. How this method of carrying on an Indian war would astonish the shades of Miles Standish and Anthony Wayne!

Saturday, 20. Orders this morning to remain in camp as a brisk rain was falling. About 8 o'clock the Crow war party arrived from over the river with startling intelligence. About noon yesterday, while reconnoitering the country from the top of the Wolf Mountains, they discovered the Sioux to the number of several hundred warriors sweeping down toward them from Tongue River. It was too late for them to fly, so they lay close and watched this formidable host defile by within a few hundred yards—all mounted and apparently equipped for war. After passing the mountains, the Sioux pushed on toward our camp till they disappeared in the Rosebud valley, when the Crows quickly descended, made a wide detour to the left, struck the river several miles above camp, crossed on a log, and hastened to us with the news.

The General, fearing for the safety of Thompson's command, immediately ordered out the remaining mounted force and five companies of infantry to proceed down the river to his relief. Captain Kirtland's company (B) was left in charge of the camp; and to expedite the march of the infantry, ten wagons were supplied to them in which the men rode by turn. Got off in about an hour and a half, in a drenching rain. My detachment as usual took the advance, scouting two or three miles across the front, and observing particularly the margin of the river for indications of a crossing by the Sioux. Passed the mouth of the Rosebud several miles, but found no sign, and as the Sioux would most likely have crossed here if anywhere, owing to the favorable character of the banks, the General became satisfied that they were still on the other side, and halted the command about nine miles below camp.

Here they bivouacked while my detachment scouted on down the river, under orders to communicate if possible with Thompson's command. Thirteen miles lower down we discovered that there was a cavalry trail leading back up the river, which induced me to believe that the cavalry companies had returned and that by taking different routes we had passed each other. I therefore turned back on this trail, finding it to lead off to the right through ravines into a broken country a mile or so from the river, and finally approach the river again through another long, deep, and devious ravine. It was surprising that the command should have taken such a course, but the mystery was soon increased by our debouching upon a cove in the bluffs where there were indications of a halt of some length having been made and several empty cartridge cases lying about on the ground. It savored somewhat of preparation for an Indian fight, but the rain had injured the sign so much that we could not form a very correct idea of its age. The approach of night put an end to our efforts to solve the puzzle, and, as the Crows confessed themselves completely at fault as to the direction the command had taken from this point, I returned to camp, arriving about an hour before midnight, without having found in the twenty-two miles we had followed the river any sign of the Sioux. The troops were in bivouac at the point they had stopped in the afternoon.

Sunday, May 21. Thompson's command arrived today, and

the mystery I had fallen upon yesterday was cleared up. It appears that on the morning of the nineteenth, the day following their departure, as they were about to move out of the timber where they had passed the night, they discovered a party of between forty and fifty Indians approaching from the direction of Tongue River, apparently with the design of crossing the river at a point some three miles above. Captain Thompson thereupon moved rapidly back under cover of the ravines and hills to the cove where I had found the empty cartridge cases and other signs of a halt, so as to bring his command directly in front of the Indians, and prepared to give them a warm reception should they cross. The Indians came down to the margin of the stream and tried the depth of the water with poles, but apparently resolved not to cross at that place and withdrew into the timber. Mitch Bouyer and one of the Crows then solicited permission to go over and try to get some of their horses, which was granted, and stripping to their skins they swam the river carrying no arms. In the timber they came on the Indians, unexpectedly, who discovered them at the same moment that they were themselves seen, and both parties fled; Bouyer and his companion recrossing the stream in all possible haste, fortunate to have escaped with their lives. Finding that the Indians would not cross, Capt. Thompson quietly withdrew his command and proceeded with his scout. He reached the mouth of Tongue River and returned without further incident and without meeting any Sioux sign, until he neared the vicinity of our camp. Here he encountered my yesterday's trail, and found that we had been followed for some distance upon our return by a small party of Sioux, whose trail approached from the river as if they had crossed a few miles below.

As the ground we bivouacked on last night appeared preferable for a permanent camp to that above, the General decided to remain and sent the wagons back this morning, accompanied by details from each company, to bring down the tents and other property. By 4 o'clock P. M. the transfer had been made, and an hour later the tents were pitched, the train corralled, and everything arranged for a lengthened stay.

I returned to the old camp with the train for the purpose of coming down the river with Captain Clifford in his boats, to enable me to land at the mouth of the Rosebud and investigate certain red-looking objects that I had discovered yesterday from the opposite shore but could not make out. They had appeared like quarters of freshly butchered meat hung upon a frame of poles, but we found them to be two Indian graves, the corpses being wrapped in red blankets and disposed in the customary manner on scaffolds, which had partly fallen down, leaving the bodies in a state of semi-suspension favorable to the delusion I had experienced. To get a better insight into the methods of Sioux burial, I perpetrated the vandalism of requesting LeForgey to tear down one of the scaffolds and pry into the arrangement and accompaniments of the corpse.

It proved to be the remains of a warrior of fifty-odd years of age, who, I should judge, had been dead about two years. His effects had been buried with him, and among them was a small package of letters, a soldier's hymn book, and a picture history of his life. The book had belonged to a soldier of some regiment of Iowa volunteers, whose name I do not remember, and among the letters were some from a wife to her absent soldier-husband, which were touching in their devotion and simplicity. Poor woman! her husband had undoubtedly never returned to her, for the possession of these souvenirs by the savages were *prima facie* evidence that the soldier had fallen in fight and been afterwards plundered of these treasured tokens of a wife's love.

There was also a paper signed "Fannie Kelly, captive white woman," whose reading touched us all to the heart and made us wish the savage was again alive that we might wreak upon him some of the indignation we felt. I cannot remember its entire contents, but it concluded by saying: "The Indians are kind to me, but I am compelled to do their bidding." "To do their bidding"! Alas, how many poor captive women have suffered this to them worse fate than death! May the end of such atrocities be near at hand! May the military operations that are now in progress result in so complete an overthrow of the hell-hounds called Sioux that never again shall poor women be made the victims of such barbarity at their hands! The name "Fanny Kelly" somehow sounded familiar to me, and for a long time I puzzled over it trying to remember why. At last it occurred to me I had somewhere read an account of her ransom a few years ago, followed afterward by an announcement that she had written and published a book of her experiences.[27]

Another object of my visit to the mouth of the Rosebud was to inspect the ruins of the old trading fort that once stood here. It bore the name of Fort Van Buren and was built by Tullock in 1839, to replace Fort Cass, situated just below the mouth of the Big Horn and abandoned the previous year. It was the second post maintained by the American Fur Co. on the Yellowstone, and enjoyed an existence of only three years when it gave way to Fort Alexander, built by Larpenteur, in 1842, on Adam's Prairie, some twenty miles higher up the Yellowstone. The accounts of the fort represent it as having been a little over a hundred feet square, and I judge from the remains, though I made no measurement, that it was. Seven ruined stone chimneys and a slight ridge where the palisades stood are all that is left of it.

[27] *My Captivity among the Sioux,* by Fanny Kelly.—W. E. S.

I recorded in my original journal of this visit: "The palisade must have been burned, as the ridge is marked with cinders and ashes"; and by an old manuscript that has fallen into my hands I find that it was, Larpenteur having set fire to it himself on the completion of his other fort. The fort stood on a plateau some eighteen or twenty feet above the present level of the water, a few yards from the bank of the Yellowstone and about seventy-five below the delta of the Rosebud.

I record these facts to assist as far as possible in lifting the early history of the fur-trading establishments on the Yellowstone from the obscurity into which it has fallen. Little Face, an old man about sixty-five years of age and a member of my detachment of Crow scouts, has told me the story of the Yellowstone posts as it has come under his own observation, having no guide in his narration but his memory; and though I listened to it and wrote it down more as a curiosity than as historic data of consequence, I have since learned to think better of it, and now deem it of value in the latter respect....[28]

It seems necessary to make some allowances for errors of memory, possibly in the number of posts given and quite certainly in the period of their duration, but in other respects the story appears in the main entitled to full credit. I have recorded it as nearly as I could in Little Face's own manner, and perhaps some who would have no interest in it as a matter of history will enjoy the charm of that portion of its original simplicity I have been able to retain.

Crow Account of the Yellowstone Fur Trade

The first traders who came to the Crows brought their goods in boats pulled up the Yellowstone by men walking on shore and hauling on a long rope which rested on their shoulders.

[28] Ellipsis indicated in original publication of the Journal.—E. I. S.

A small party of Crows scouting below the mouth of the Big Horn first discovered the boat and saw that the men were very tired and their clothes worn through on their shoulders where the rope rested. So they hastened to the village, which was then hunting near the mountains about the headwaters of the Rosebud and Stillwater [Stillwater Fork and its branches], and informed their friends that traders were coming, and that they were very tired and needed horses to help them along. The Crows then took some of their best horses and mules and went to meet the boat, supposing that the traders would unload the boat and pack their goods on the animals; but instead of that they hitched the horses and mules to the boat and kept on in it nearly to the mouth of the Big Horn, where, on the right bank of the Yellowstone about two miles below the mouth of the Big Horn, they stopped to trade.

Here the trader made presents of looking-glasses to the Crows who had helped him, and sent word to the village that he had come a long way to trade with them for robes, of which he hoped they would dress a great many the next winter. The traders made a circular breastwork of logs to put their goods in, in which they were staying when the Crows left to go to their village. There were about forty of the traders, and the principal man was the Crane [Tullock].

The Crows were glad to have a trader in their country and resolved to make a good hunt and give him a big trade. Before this they had never dressed more robes than they needed for themselves, but this winter they went to Wind River, where the buffalo were plenty, and killed a good many, and dressed all the robes, so that every lodge had from sixteen to eighteen robes to sell to the trader. There were plenty of Crows in those days. The next spring they came down and found that the traders had put up buildings of logs and made a fort, and were all ready to trade.

The Crane told the Crows that he had come a long way with his goods, and that it had been very hard work for him to get there, and that he wanted the Crows to give him good prices for his goods. He asked seven robes for a flint-lock gun with a red stock, nine robes for a percussion-lock gun with a speckled stock, one robe for a powder-horn filled with powder, seven and nine robes for two kinds of striped blankets, six robes for a red blanket, five robes for a purple blanket, four robes for a blue blanket, three robes for a white or green blanket, and eight robes for a beautiful red coat trimmed with gold and silver lace on the breast and sleeves, the skirts of which reached below the knees. These coats were the finest things ever brought into the Crow country. These were the principal things the Crane had to trade, but he had also a great many small articles, as beads, knives, wire, looking-glasses, etc., which he gave as presents to those who sold him robes. Besides the robes, the Crane told them to bring him good sound elkhorns, which he bought of them to take away for knife handles. He bought a good many elkhorns.

The Crows kept on making robes to sell, and the Crane stayed in their country for seven snows [years], when he said he must go back down the river, but would return some day. So he loaded all his robes in his boats, burned down his fort, and sailed off. The Crows kept a lookout for him, but he was gone three snows, and, when he came back, had horses to pull his boats, and stopped at the mouth of the Rosebud to build his fort. The Crows were camped on the Little Big Horn, but the Crane packed some things on horses and came to the camp. The things that he brought were for presents, and he did not trade any there. It was in the fall that the traders came to the Rosebud; and the next spring the Crows came over and found that they had built a fort.

The Crane did not stay long, but left another man, Big Nose, in his place. The Crane went away east, among the white people, and never came back. He had two wives among the Crows, whom he left when he went away, and several children, only one of whom he took away with him. He was a tall, slender man with long sandy hair. The Crows did not like Big Nose because he was rude to them in trade, often throwing their robes back into their faces when they were not tanned soft enough to suit him. So they told him they did not want any such men to trade with them, and that he must take his goods out of their country, and he did so after the fort had been at the Rosebud for three snows.

Three snows after the Rosebud fort was abandoned, Round Iron [Meldrum] came to trade with them. The Crows liked Round Iron. He was the best white man that ever came to the Crow country. He could speak Crow like one of themselves, and no one could tell from his talk that he was not a Crow. He had first come to their country when he was a boy and had grown up among them. Round Iron had four posts among the Crows, the first was on the Big Horn just above the mouth of the Little Big Horn,[29] where he stayed three snows; the second was on the right bank of the Yellowstone, nearly opposite but a little above the mouth of the Great Porcupine, where he stayed two snows; the third was on the same side of the Yellowstone, a few miles lower down, where he stayed five snows; and the last was on the left bank of the

[29] There is some doubt as to whether this fort was really built by Round Iron (Meldrum), and likewise as to the location of the fort said to have been built at the mouth of the Big Horn by Manuel Lisa. One map now in existence locates Lisa's or Manuel's fort at or near the mouth of Tongue River. As good an authority as the late A. M. Quivey declared he had found traces of a fort a number of miles above the mouth of the Big Horn, near where the Little Big Horn empties into that stream, and believed them to mark the site of Manuel Lisa's fort, supposed to have been built at the mouth of the Big Horn by him in 1807. He never could find any traces of a fort at or near the mouth of the Big Horn.—H. S. W.

Yellowstone, between the Rosebud and Tongue Rivers, where he stayed four snows.

While he was at the latter place, an opposition fort was built on the same side of the river close to his own—in fact the two forts were almost together. The man who built the opposition fort was a Crow, but I do not remember his name. When the opposition fort had been there two snows, a great flood came on the Yellowstone that filled the whole valley full of water and made it look like one big river from one bluff to the other. The two trading forts were surrounded and filled with water, which wet the robes and goods and frightened the traders so much that they loaded everything on their boats and went away.

Round Iron went first, when the river began to threaten them, but the opposition trader stayed until the water went down, and then left in the fall. These were the last posts on the Yellowstone.

Round Iron went down to the fort at the mouth of the Yellowstone, which had been there a long time;[30] and the Crows have been told that he there got to drinking whisky so much that he died. The fort built by the Crane at the mouth of the Big Horn is the first that I know of. It was built two snows before the stars fell. I was then a boy, but almost a man. I have heard there was another fort there a long time ago, but it was before my time, and I can tell nothing about it.

Monday, 22. Three cavalrymen while hunting in the hills back of camp were fired upon by Indians and retreated to the camp. Wheelan's company and my detachment were ordered out to pursue the Indians, he going down stream and I up, the Crows who could get a mount taking a middle course. I turned into the hills to the right two miles up and made a wide detour around the camp, meeting the Crows, who had

30 Fort Union.—E. I. S.

MAJOR MARCUS A. RENO

"CAMP OF SITTING BULL IN THE BIG HORN MOUNTAINS"
from a painting by Henry H. Cross, 1873.

found the trail of eight or ten Sioux. We attempted to follow it but soon found that they had scattered, when we lost it completely. Traveled so rapidly that two of my horses gave out. Described a circuit of about twenty-four miles, returning to the camp at 5:30 P. M. without seeing Indians or discovering any further sign. Wheelan was equally unsuccessful, and returned about the same time.

Tuesday, 23. Company I (Lieut. English) left at 7:30 A. M., as escort to the contract train of John W. Power, which has been discharged, E. G. Maclay & Co. having been awarded the contract for hauling in Montana this year. English takes one Gatling gun, and is accompanied by Lieut. Johnson. Bravo and two of the Crows go along for the purpose of visiting the Crow village to procure horses for the dismounted Crows, all but two having agreed to send for them. Lieutenant English will continue on with the discharged train until he meets the "Diamond R"[31] supply train now en route from Fort Ellis under charge of Lieutenant Kendrick, when he will send Power's wagons on, returning in charge of the supply train to this camp, where we will remain until rejoined by him. Company F, 2nd Cavalry (Lieut. Roe), left with Lieutenant English and will travel with him for two days and will then return, as it is considered that the train will then be out of danger.

Citizen Herendeen, while out hunting this morning a couple of miles from camp, heard rapid firing in the hills and saw Indians at the point where it occurred, and as a small hunting party had gone in that direction he believed them attacked, and hurried in with the news. Companies G, H and L of the cavalry were ordered out at once in that direction, finding at the distance of three miles from camp the bodies of Privates Raymeyer and Stoker, Company H, 2d Cavalry, and Citizen-

[31] The name of a famous freighting outfit of early times.

Teamster Quinn, riddled with balls, and Stoker scalped. The Sioux had ambuscaded them in a ravine and probably killed two of them instantly, but the other had evidently fired several shots in his defense, before he was entirely dispatched, and, it is thought, killed one Indian, as they marked the body in the manner that they are said to do in such cases—by sticking their knives into the head. The Indians had decamped, carrying off an infantry rifle and two cavalry carbines and pistols, with which the men had been armed. Company L returned with the bodies, while Companies G and H pursued the trail of the Indians, who from the indications number about 40, but farther on traces were found of from 150 to 200 men. As usual the Indians baffled pursuit by scattering so as to leave no trail and the companies returned towards evening. The bodies were interred with military honors at 7 P.M.

It should be added that these unfortunate men were absent from the camp without permission, though the same thing is liable to happen any day to parties absent with permission. The General gives hunting passes freely, believing that the experience is good for the men and that it is as good a system of scouting as could be devised for the vicinity of the camp.

Little Face, in telling me the history of Tattooed Forehead, a celebrated Crow chief of early times, narrated the following incident:

Tattooed Forehead once approached a camp of Assiniboines, enemies of the Crows, feigning idiocy and so disguised that he appeared like one of their own tribe. It chanced that two young women had sought a secluded nook on the banks of an adjacent stream, and having laid aside their clothes, were disporting naked in the water. They discovered the approach of Tattooed Forehead, but, supposing him to be one of their own village, suffered only the alarm natural to modest maidens at the prospect of being discovered in such a state by one of the other sex, and sought shelter in the nearest bushes until he should go by. Pretending to pass on, Tattooed Forehead drew near them from behind unperceived, and as they, believing themselves undiscovered, were softly laughing and joking over the adventure, he suddenly protruded his arm through the bushes and seized one of them by the long hair which hung around her shoulders. Ere they could recover from their amazement the other hand followed, clasping a glittering knife, and in an instant the poor girl's head was severed from her body, her companion fleeing with screams of terror. Some of our Crows, and among them Little Face, shed tears today over the fate of our three unfortunate men, giving their blankets to bury them in; and in the course of my acquaintance with him, Little Face has given many other proofs of a gentle disposition and kind heart. It is therefore an excellent illustration of the degree to which the hearts of even the best-disposed Indians are hardened toward their enemies and their natures brutalized, that the fate of this poor, innocent maiden, under circumstances so revolting to civilized perceptions, actually appeared to Little Face a good joke and caused him in the telling of it to chuckle with delight.

Colonel Chestnut, a Bozeman gentleman, arrived today in a mackinaw boat, bringing a cargo of vegetables, butter, eggs, tobacco, and other goods. He had a crew of four men, and had made the run from Bensen's [*sic*] Landing without seeing any Sioux or meeting with any misadventure. The luxuries he brought found ready sale and gave great satisfaction. Not the least acceptable article was a keg of beer, reserved for the officers and resulting in a convivial reunion in the evening at the tent of Lieutenant Hamilton and Schofield. It gave tongue to hitherto voiceless eloquence, inspired to polemical contests of racy sort, and put the voices of our singers once more in splendid tune. The time passed jollily, Colonel Chestnut was voted the best fellow going, and the occasion will long be remembered as one of the greenest of the green spots in the campaign.

Several Indians rode into view on the opposite side of the river just before dark, one of them wearing an immense war-bonnet, which he shook at us defiantly. They were about a mile distant, and after surveying us for a few minutes rode away. It was thought that the camp might be fired on tonight from the opposite side of the river, and as a preparation there-for, the twelve-pounder was after dark rolled up near the bank convenient to reply. Each company has been assigned a position to be taken in case of attack, and, as Indian attacks usually occur just before day, we are hereafter to form thereon about 2 o'clock, remaining until broad daylight.

Wednesday, 24–Friday, 26. During these three days we have remained quietly in camp, occupied by day principally in trying to keep cool, the weather having been very hot. On the twenty-fourth a strange horse was seen below camp about a half mile distant, and Lieutenant Coolidge with ten soldiers and three Crows were sent down to investigate the cause of its presence. Upon their approach a Sioux appeared in view, mounted the horse and fled, making good his escape. These rascals have a good deal of a certain kind of boldness. Lieu-tenant Roe's company (F) returned at 10 A. M. on the twenty-sixth, having accompanied Lieutenant English to within two miles of our camp of the tenth inst.—about twenty miles below Fort Pease. Had seen no Indian sign. About 11 A. M. on the twenty-sixth the planet Venus was discovered shining with a pale light, and continued visible through the remainder of the day. The day was intensely bright, the sun shining from a cloudless sky, and the appearance of the star excited general wonder. I identified it as Venus by observing later in the day that it was the evening star. The moon was between five and six degrees distant from it, nearer the western horizon, and served as a guide to finding the star.

Saturday, 27. I was sent with my detachment on a scout over the river this morning to see what had become of the Indians, none of whom have appeared in view during the last few days. Captain Clifford went over with his company soon after daylight to occupy the bluffs and support me in case I had to fall back, and as soon as he was through with the boats, I crossed my command, swimming the horses. Made the crossing in about half an hour, all being over by 5 o'clock. I had with me thirteen men of my mounted detachment, Le Forgey and five Crows—twenty including myself. Passing up the river about a mile, we entered a deep, dry ravine, which we followed for several miles till it ran out some three or four miles from the base of the Little Wolf Mountains, and then crossed the plains to the mountains, heading for the point from which we had made our observations on the sixteenth inst. After leaving the ravine, the country afforded no opportunity for concealment, which made it rather ticklish business exposing ourselves in such small force.

As we pushed on, we were forcibly reminded of the danger of such an excursion by the abundant Indian sign we found on every hand. The country was dotted thickly with the carcasses of freshly killed buffalo, the hides all having been removed in the manner it is done when they are designed for lodge-skins. The pony tracks were innumerable, showing that there must have been hundreds of mounted Indians here within a recent period. Near the mountains, where they had been compelled to travel close together to pass defiles, they left a beaten track like a traveled road. The tracks appeared to be generally about a week old, though there were some of much later date, and the carcasses had been exposed for about the same period. All this goes to show that the Crows did not report falsely when they claimed to have seen from the top of the mountains an army of Sioux warriors pass by toward the Rosebud on the nineteenth inst.

After a four hours' march, having traveled some fourteen miles, we reached the foot of the hills at the same place we struck them on the sixteenth, and leaving the detachment in the same sheltered cove, I ascended with the Crows to our old point of lookout to take a survey of the country. We had no sooner reached the summit than we discovered smoke on the Rosebud River, and, bringing our glasses to bear upon it, found ourselves again in the vicinity of an immense Indian camp. In numerous places up and down the valley the smoke was rising in columns and blending in a cloud over the camp, the break in the bluffs revealed the tops of several lodges—in a few instances, the entire lodge. The plain above the camp was dotted with hundreds of moving black specks that could only be horses, and while we gazed, there came distinctly to our ears from the broken ground at the base of the hills the sounds of several rifle shots, showing that the Sioux hunters were at work.

Feeling sure that my line of retreat was open, I made no haste to return, but passed about half an hour watching the camp and studying the probabilities. When I passed here on the sixteenth, there was no sign of a camp on the Rosebud, and it therefore appeared probable that the village we had discovered on Tongue River had since moved over. Then they were about thirty-five miles from our command, but now they were only eighteen; and the fact that they had moved down within easy striking distance seemed to prove that they held us in no awe. This movement probably took place on the nineteenth inst., and the body of Sioux warriors seen by the four Crows were merely the advance guard of the camp designed to cover its march. As near as I could estimate, the village was about eight, possibly ten, miles from our lookout, so that objects appeared indistinct, and I could not have felt sure that the animals in sight were not buffalo but for the attendant circumstances. But there was no doubt about the shots, the lodges, and the smoke, and to the Indians none about the animals, their better-trained eyes distinguishing them readily as horses and enabling them to make out the most decided colors.

While we watched, a large band of horses were driven down into the valley apparently to water, and after awhile reappeared and spread themselves over the plain. This movement was made so deliberately that it excited no apprehension on our part; but, soon after, another took place that looked like a hurried catching up of the horses, which made us think that possibly scouts had reported our presence, and a party was making up to look after us. The Crows felt sure that this was the case, and, as we were about as far from our camp as they were, there was a chance of their getting in behind us and cutting us off unless we made good time back. The Crows had been very cool up to this moment, but now they got terribly excited, and when I told them I wanted to bring my men up where they could see the camp, too, they protested against it most earnestly, insisting that we had not a moment to lose. I went back to the command, told them what we had seen, and offered them the opportunity to go up and take a look at the camp if they wanted to, but they all said it would please them better to get out as quickly as possible. I was rather anxious they should see it, because upon our return from our first scout there had been some parties ungenerous enough to deny that we had found a village, and I wanted to accumulate testimony.[32]

[32] This is one of the few places where the hard feeling between some of the officers of Gibbon's command is apparent.—E. I. S.

Having got started upon our return, I considered it best to make good time, and we were only two hours in going a distance we had been five in coming, getting back to the river at 11:30 A.M. Having crossed and reported to the General, I was ordered to bring back my detachment and effected the crossing in almost half an hour, Captain Clifford's company remaining over until dark.

Everybody wondered why we were not ordered over to attack the village; but the General probably had good reasons. The village was only eighteen miles distant, we had half a day to cross in, and by leaving the horses behind, could have been over the river ready to begin the march at dark, when we would easily have reached the village before day. The absence of Lieutenant English's company left us with an available force of only about 350 men, and whether that was enough to have attacked successfully is uncertain. It was subsequently ascertained that the village contained about 400 lodges, representing a fighting force of between 800 and 1,000 warriors. It was pretty big odds, but I imagine the majority of our officers would not have hesitated to give them a trial, and there are some who assert confidently that we would have gained a rousing victory, dispersed the village, and prevented that tremendous aggregation of force a month later that made the massacre of Custer's command possible. On the other hand, we might ourselves have been massacred.

As it is thought that General Terry will by this time have reached the vicinity of Glendive Creek or Powder River, General Gibbon has for a day or two been preparing to send despatches to him by way of the river. A skiff was put in good order, supplied with extra oars and with padded oar-locks, and this evening, just after dark, sailed on its venturesome voyage, the crew consisting of citizen Williamson and two soldiers of Captain Clifford's company, Bell and Stewart, who had volunteered for the service. They will keep a careful look-out for Custer's column, and if they fail to strike it, continue on down the river to Fort Buford,[33] or until they meet one of the steamers. About the same time that the boat put off, Ball's and Thompson's companies marched for Tongue River, to scout the country in that direction and look after the boat.

Sunday, 28. Mr. McCormick, accompanied by two men, arrived today in a mackinaw, bringing a cargo of vegetables, butter, tobacco, cigars, canned goods, etc., and a large mail. They saw no Sioux and met with no accident. It is understood that General Gibbon has received new orders from General Terry. The hostiles are reported concentrating in large numbers at Glendive Creek, and we are to march to that point to co-operate with the forces now en route from Fort Abraham Lincoln. It will be impossible to do so until we are joined by the supply train that Lieutenant English is bringing down; and to facilitate its arrival, every available wagon here is to be sent back tomorrow to meet and lighten it. Captain Sanno will go in charge of them, taking as escort his own company and Lieutenant Roe's.

The day was passed in getting the train and escort ready for an early start in the morning. It is exceedingly unlikely that such a concentration is taking place for the village opposite us is apparently working the other way, having already crossed from Tongue River to the Rosebud.

Monday, 29. Captain Sanno's command got off this morning. The officers with him are Lieutenants Jacobs, Woodruff, and Roe. He has twenty-four wagons and took two of the Crow scouts. About 2 P. M., Captain Ball's command arrived from Tongue River; they found no recent Sioux sign, and did

---

[33] At the confluence of the Yellowstone and Missouri rivers. First garrisoned in 1866, it was occupied at this time by the Sixth Infantry under Colonel William Hazen.—E. I. S.

not see the dispatch boat. In McCormick's cargo was a limited quantity of whisky and champagne cider, and convivial re-unions are a natural consequence. Some of the gentlemen concocted a new drink that speedily won favor. In consid-eration of our near vicinity to the stream of that name, it re-ceived the pleasant appellation of "Rosebud." It continued a favorite throughout the campaign, or as long as the in-gredients lasted, and ever since the return of the expedition old memories are occasionally revived by a recurrence thereto.

Tuesday, 30. Two of the Crows this evening made another of those abortive attempts at horse stealing, for which they have distinguished themselves since they have been with us. They were carried over the river just before dark, and passed out of view in the gathering gloom, but not long afterward were discovered on the bank of the river calling lustily for a boat, announcing that the Sioux were close at hand. A squad was drawn up under arms along the bank to cover the advance of the boat, which was hurried over with all possible speed, and the Crows were soon safe on this side. Their story was that, when first set over, they advanced toward the bluffs, fancying they saw moving objects in their front, which in-duced them to proceed with the utmost caution. Entering a ravine, they followed it up till they reached the top of the bluffs, but had no sooner done so than to their consternation they perceived about thirty mounted Sioux near at hand com-ing directly toward them. Discovery seemed inevitable, but at that moment two others appeared from a different direc-tion, and, meeting the main party, all halted and conferred together for some time but a few yards distant from the crouching and trembling Crows. Then they turned off and disappeared from view in a neighboring ravine, and, as soon as they could safely move, the Crows made all possible haste back to the river. It turns out that we have not wanted any

Sioux villages, but had it been otherwise, it seems likely that we would have continued to want them for all that the Crows would have found for us. They are mortally afraid of the Sioux, and, even when they pluck up courage and start, the slightest misadventure suffices to convince them that their "medicine" is bad, and then back they come.

Wednesday, 31. Wheelan's company, accompanied by Le-Forgey and five Crows, made a scout up the river to the distance of sixteen miles, starting soon after daybreak and returning about 5 P.M., without having seen any sign of Sioux.

The Yellowstone has been rising rapidly for many days and is now very high. A measurement of the channel at this point makes its breadth a little over three hundred yards.

To show how our gentlemen are amusing themselves I quote the journal of one of them: "Up all night playing 'Pedro' for eggs." When the attack was made on Baker's command in 1872, it found several gentlemen wide awake and absorbed in the mysteries of "poker," from which circumstance the fight is sometimes jocularly called the "Battle of Poker Flat." Being already dressed, they were quickly at their posts; and judging by this precedent, there seems little objection to these egg-hungry disciples of "Pedro" giving, if they choose to, the benefit of their night vigils to those of us who prefer to sleep. We can slumber in greater security, knowing that an assemblage of grim-visaged and valiant warriors sit ready at the first alarm to throw themselves into the breach and give time to the rest of us to throw ourselves into our breeches.

Thusday, June 1–Saturday, 3. On the first instant it snowed most of the day, melting as it fell but accumulating to the depth of about one inch toward evening. It continued stormy through the following night, and upon the second inst. was so cold all day that fires were necessary to comfort. The cold had the effect of reducing the flow of water in the mountain tributaries of the Yellowstone and the river fell two and a half feet in three days.

An effort was made on the second inst. to induce the Crows to form a war party to go to the Sioux village after horses; but after deliberating awhile, they decided that the moon is too bright—that is, the nights are not dark enough to conceal their movements.

On the third inst. Captain Ball's company marched up the river to the Great Porcupine to look out a good crossing for the train and bridge that and other streams wherever necessary.

Sunday, 4. Captain Logan's company bridged a dry creek about three miles below camp, putting up a substantial log bridge of two spans. At 2 P. M. the long-looked-for Diamond R supply train rolled into camp, and our command is all together again. Matt. Carroll,[34] of the firm of E. G. Maclay & Co., comes in charge of the train and is an agreeable addition to our circle of associates. It will be remembered that, when in April the supply camp below Stillwater Fork was abandoned, Lieutenant Kendrick went on to Fort Ellis in charge of certain discharged contract wagons. He arrived there on the fifth day of May, the fourteenth of May set out on his return in charge of the Diamond R contract train of ten wagons, carrying 100,000 pounds of freight, his original escort strengthened by a detail of fifteen infantrymen from the garrison of Fort Ellis. Six miles below Baker's battle ground, on the twenty-eighth of May, he met the train and escort commanded by Lieutenant English, who then sent the discharged train on to Fort Ellis, escorted by the detail of fifteen men that had accompanied Lieutenant Kendrick from that post, and turned about with his company. Being the senior officer, he relieved Lieutenant Kendrick of the charge of the Diamond R train

---

[34] For his diary of this campaign, see *Contributions to the Historical Society of Montana,* II (1896).—E. I. S.

and continued in command until the thirtieth of May, when, fifteen miles below Pompey's Pillar, he was met by the train which, under the command of Captain Sanno, was going up to his assistance. The Diamond R train was then lightened by loading a portion of the stores on the empty train brought by Captain Sanno, who assumed command of the whole and conducted it to our camp, meeting Ball's company at the Great Porcupine yesterday, which returned with him.

The march of all these columns had been without special incident except the unfortunate killing of Sergeant Belicke of Company C, 7th Infantry. He was a member of the additional escort furnished at Fort Ellis to Lieutenant Kendrick upon the return trip, and while camped near Little Timber Creek seems in making the rounds of the sentinels after dark to have gotten unintentionally outside of the line. He was challenged by a sentinel in the abominable manner practiced in this command—by whistling—but failed to respond, when the sentinel, supposing him an enemy, fired, killing him instantly. He was buried near the place he fell—a victim to this wretched method of challenging. There could be but one thing worse: to fire on sight without challenging at all. By either method we would kill about a hundred of our men to one Indian, but, though it would be rather unpleasant to have murdered the hundred in this way, there would be a deal of satisfaction in having got away with that solitary red-skin.

Bravo and his two Crows returned with the train, having been successful in getting horses for the dismounted Crows, so that once more all are provided with a mount except the two who would not send for one. The sight of their comrades comfortably seated in the saddle, curveting and prancing in high glee, makes these two obstreperous fellows feel very crestfallen. They might have had horses also, but for a fit of Indian obstinacy or ill-humor that induced them to throw away the opportunity to send for them. Bravo is entitled to great credit for this service, as it was attended with considerable risk. He left the command at Pompey's Pillar on its up trip, swam the Yellowstone where the water was almost icy cold, sought the Crow village at a venture—uncertain where to find it—luckily reached it, got his horses, and set out on his return, overtaking the command on its return trip about twenty miles below Fort Pease—all this in country where he was constantly liable to come in contact with the Sioux. We are under orders to march tomorrow.

Monday, 5. Since the twenty-fourth ult. we have turned out about 2 o'clock in the morning and lain on our arms in line until broad daylight, but this morning the practice was discontinued—much to the satisfaction of everybody. Reveille is appointed for 3:30. Marched at 8:55 A. M., keeping down the valley, and camped at 1:30 P. M., having advanced nine miles. Soon after we halted, the General and his party routed a bear out of the thicket near camp, and after a short chase the General killed it. He caused it to be butchered, and distributed the meat to several of the officers' messes, giving to many their first experience of such fare. It was quite palatable and strongly suggestive of fresh pork. Our camp is beautifully located near a chute of the river, groves of timber near at hand and long green grass beneath our feet. It was only half a mile from here that Captain Thompson's command lay in wait in the hills for the party of Sioux who attempted to cross on the nineteenth of May.

The afternoon was very warm, but by rolling up the sides of the tents and admitting the slight air stirring, it was pleasant enough. It looked more like picnicking than going to war, to see officers and men comfortably reclining in the shade reading books and newspapers, writing letters, posting diaries, playing cards, talking, or dozing "the happy hours away," according to their individual moods. And the picnic impression was heightened when, later in the afternoon, the supper was made ready on the grass and hungry groups gathered here and there over cups of steaming, savory coffee and other fare. Nor was coffee the only beverage. From the capacious recesses of secure mess-chests came forth at odd times nutmeg, lemon, sugar, Angostura bitters, champagne cider, and *spiritus frumenti,* from which were made tempting "Rosebuds," cocktails, toddies, and other harmless compounds. When each member of the charmed circle had been duly supplied, the master of ceremonies would briefly announce, "Here's How!" and, with a chorus of "Hows" from his co-laborers, the exhilarating compounds were gently put where they would do the most good.

In the dusk of evening, when most of the officers were gathered in front of some of the tents, a chorus of cavalrymen not far away burst forth with a round of merry camp songs, that came pleasantly to the ear and suspended for a time the conversation upon battles we haven't fought and victories we haven't won. And when "taps" impose silence upon the enlisted men, the officers, who enjoyed larger liberties, took up the suspended harmony and woke the night air with many a song of sentiment and jollity. We have a number of very sweet singers in our command, and the music at times is of a delicious sort. But rest is needful for the march of tomorrow and after a time the group of singers and listeners broke up with a mutual "good night," tents are sought, sleep settles upon the camp, and all is quiet upon the Yellowstone. Not even a sentinel is visible, for, disposed in groups of three around us for some distance from the camp, they are all lying flat upon the ground with nothing to mark their locality. It is hard to realize when about the camp that we are an invading army, liable at any moment to be engaged in deadly conflict with a cruel foe. I presume to few except myself has a sense of danger come home at all, and to me only when exposed with a handful of men miles from the command.

Tuesday, 6. I left camp with my detachment and the Indians at 8 A.M., getting a good start ahead of the command, which followed an hour later. It took the train three hours to get up the hill, at the foot of which our last night's camp was pitched. Finding myself several miles ahead of the command, I halted, posted sentinels, and unsaddled, remaining several hours before the command appeared. At one time there occurred rapid firing on the river which excited a momentary apprehension that the boats had been attacked; but it proved to be Captain Clifford and men firing upon elk, one of which they killed and secured. After crossing the high grounds for a distance of some three miles, the road entered the valley again. After a march of ten miles we turned off to the river and camped, at 4 P.M., in a beautiful cottonwood grove on splendid sod. In the evening we were treated to a high wind that roared grandly through the trees. It came up suddenly and for a time threatened a general conflagration, as it set troops of burning coals hopping through the camp from the cook fires and deluged the tents with sparks. While this display of fireworks was going on, the gloom was rent with lightning flashes, and the low rumble of distant thunder swelled on the air. There was a sublimity in the scene that produced a strong impression on many minds. There was a drawback to its enjoyment, however, in the tossing boughs that threatened destruction to the tents pitched beneath them and the necessity of manning the poles to keep the tents from going down before the blast.

Wednesday, 7. Marched at 7:45 A.M., continued down the valley a few miles, then ascended to the highlands which abut on the river for several miles above and below the mouth

Roahen photograph

THE VALLEY OF THE LITTLE BIG HORN.

"Graves" of unknown soldiers on the ridge where the last stand was made on Custer's battlefield on the Little Big Horn.

of Tongue River. Toward evening turned to the right and approaching the river descended to a small patch of valley, where we pitched camp at 7 P. M., having marched twenty-two miles. The descent to the valley was by a difficult ravine, where the wagons lost half an hour. It was 9 o'clock before the camp was fairly in shape and half an hour later before suppers were ready, by which time there were four hundred very hungry men. Found a clear, cold spring in the bluffs about a mile from camp, but it furnished a very limited supply of water.

Thursday, 8. Took the advance as usual with my detachment and the Crows, the command following at 7 A. M. Had gained the valley of a nameless creek a few miles below camp, when from the hills in front came the wolf cry that indicated a discovery by the Crows in advance. The Crows rapidly rallied on the detachment, and we prepared for fight, but fortunately were not called upon to do so. The occasion of the signal was that one of the Crows had found a trail of two shod horses leading down the river, and, following it a short distance, came upon a seamless sack lying on the ground, which he picked up and brought back without opening. I caused it to be opened and found the contents to be a quantity of sugar, tea, bacon, crackers, hard bread, butter, and cartridges, several of the articles being wrapped in pieces of newspaper. They were such supplies as were likely to have belonged only to white men, and the fact that the horses were shod made it pretty evident that the owners were white men, the fresh character of the provisions indicate that they had only quite recently quitted a steamboat or large camp. It seemed probable that they were couriers from General Terry, who, discovering our Indians, supposed them to be Sioux and fled, either losing the sack or throwing it away because it impeded their flight. A further examination of the trail disclosed that it first came up the river valley and then, turning to the right into the hills, doubled on its former course.

Sent back a written report of the circumstance to General Gibbon and then moved on, took position on a high, flat, detached hill, standing near the river, from which we had a wide view of the surrounding country, unsaddled, and waited three hours for the command to come up. A couple of miles lower down, the command halted for two hours in a grove on the river bank, then moved on for six miles, and camped near the river at 7:40 P. M., having marched sixteen miles. The valley is here quite extensive, being some three miles wide and at least fifteen long, but is almost entirely destitute of timber. We had great difficulty in finding wood enough for cooking purposes, but a friendly drift in the river helped us out. The grass is heavy but provokingly matted with prickly pears, so that it was impossible to pitch tents in line. A considerable rapid spans the river a few rods below our camp.[35]

As it was expected that we would have to camp tonight on the highlands at some distance from the river, Captain Clifford was directed to take two days' rations in his boats to be prepared for a separation from the main command. It was the General's intention that he should make only about the usual run and go into camp, so as to be as near the command as possible; but a mistake was made in the delivery of the order and Captain Clifford understood himself to be at liberty to make the two days' march in one run, and so passed on with the intention of fortifying at the mouth of Powder River, there awaiting our arrival. He is accompanied by Major Brisbin and Lieutenant Doane.[36]

[35] Probably Buffalo Rapids, so named by Captain William Clark.—E. I. S.

[36] Lieutenant Gustavus C. Doane, Second Cavalry. In addition to his services in the Indian wars he was later a member of the Howgate Expedition to the Arctic.—E. I. S.

Friday, 9. About 2 A.M., citizen Herendeen and a Crow Indian, who had accompanied Captain Clifford yesterday in the boats, arrived in camp with dispatches from General Terry. At Powder River, Captain Clifford had met the steamer "Far West" and soon afterward General Terry himself, who came in with two companies of the 7th Cavalry. Learning that our column was so near, the General at once sent back orders to General Gibbon to leave his command in camp and come down himself to meet the boat, which would continue on up the river till the meeting took place. About 7 A.M. the General started, preceded by my detachment and the Crows and accompanied by Ball's company as escort. About eight miles down we met the boat, it having on board General Terry and staff and Captain Clifford's company. General Gibbon went on board, and General Terry, finding that our camp was so near, passed on up the river with the boat, Captain Ball and myself returning by the way we came. We reached the camp about noon, and soon afterward the boat arrived, landing opposite the camp. General Terry invited all the officers to meet him on board. After a stay of about two hours the boat was cleared and returned down the river.

The arrival of the 7th Cavalry at Glendive Creek disproved the reported gathering of the hostiles in that quarter, and our whole force is now to push up the river after the village we had first discovered in Tongue River and afterward on the Rosebud. The 7th Cavalry under Custer will scour the country south of the Yellowstone, while we return up the north bank to prevent the Indians from escaping to this side. As it is feared they may attempt to do so, the four companies of the 2nd Cavalry were placed under orders to move back at once, and would have got off today had not a heavy rain set in, accompanied by hail, which caused the movement to be suspended until tomorrow. The infantry will soon follow, and we will then go into camp near the mouth of the Rosebud to await further orders. Meantime the steamer returns to Glendive Creek, to bring up the stores left there to Powder River.

The trail we found yesterday had been made, as we surmised, by couriers from General Terry—Williamson and a companion, who had been promised two hundred dollars if they went through. They had been frightened back by the sight of our Crows, and so lost their two hundred dollars at the moment it was earned. Williamson made the run down from our camp near Rosebud without difficulty and safely delivered his dispatches.

On our way back to camp today after meeting the boat, LeForgey, one of my interpreters, had a fall from his horse while chasing antelope, breaking his collar bone. I was compelled to leave him where he fell, in charge of two of my men, till an ambulance could be sent for him. He appeared to mind the fracture but little, and in the evening was walking around camp.

Saturday, 10. It rained all last night and continued through the forenoon. The road is exceedingly muddy; but the cavalry marched at 3 P.M., under command of Major Brisbin. Bravo and six Crows accompanied them. The infantry are under orders to march tomorrow, moving at 7 o'clock.

Sunday, June 11. Marched at 6:20 A.M., forty minutes ahead of time. Made rather slow progress, as the road was heavy from recent rains. About 10 o'clock reached the nameless creek that enters the Yellowstone six or seven miles below Tongue River, and found it swelled to the dimensions of a river. It took two hours to make one crossing, whereas on our way down we crossed it three times without difficulty. We here came in sight of the cavalry, whose train was toiling slowly up the steep hill on the opposite side of the creek, having been compelled to seek a new road, as the rise of the creek had rendered the regular road impassable. About noon we were all over and the train was corralled, and the mules turned out to graze, while a large working party fell to, to make a new road up the hill just below the point where the cavalry wagons made their difficult ascent. The work had scarcely begun when a heavy rain set in, suspending our labors and compelling us to form camp for the night.

The maps give no name to this creek and nobody in the command had ever heard a name for it, so our engineering officer, Lieutenant McClernand, christened it quite appropriately Mud Creek. The water is horribly muddy and all attempts to settle it failed. It answered neither for cooking nor washing, and we might also as well have been camped in a desert. Vinegar cleared it somewhat, and the addition of lemon-sugar made a fairly palatable lemonade that quenched thirst.

Monday, 12. Broke camp at 6 A. M., and consumed three and a half hours getting the train up the hill at a cost of one wagon overturned. It was righted and reloaded, the damage having been slight. Once up, we made good time across the plateau opposite Tongue River, where the road was level and dry. This plateau is between ten and twelve miles long and about three miles wide, crowding up the Yellowstone on the one side and breaking into bad-lands on the other. The plateau itself is generally quite level and clothed with fine grass. Stanley's quadruple trail of 1873 is distinctly marked throughout its whole length. I rode over and took a look into Tongue River valley. It is heavily clothed with timber as far up as the eye could reach. The mouth of Tongue River was not in sight, as the stream made a sharp curve to the right and entered the Yellowstone under a screen of timber. The latter stream here washes the base of the bluffs on the north side, the valley being wholly confined to the opposite shore.

As we reached the upper end of the plateau, we caught a glimpse of the cavalry about eight miles in front. We descended into the valley and camped at 7 P.M. at the foot of the hill, three miles from the river having marched sixteen miles. We obtained water from stagnant pools and used sagebrush for fuel. The discovery of an occasional rattlesnake in camp enlivens our stay here.

Tuesday, 13. Marched at 7 A. M. The road was quite heavy, being largely a sticky clay, and we made slow progress. At 1 P. M. we halted at a creek and passed two hours making a crossing place for the wagons; but even with this precaution broke two wagons in crossing and tipped one of them over in a ditch. After a march of only thirteen miles, camped at 4 P. M. at the upper extremity of the valley across which our road has been today.

Wednesday, 14. Broke camp at 7 A. M., entered the coulee opposite camp, crossed the three-mile-wide ridge, descended into the valley above, and followed it up nearly to our old Rosebud camp, where after a march of twelve miles we pitched camp at 2 P. M., a few hundred yards above the cavalry, who arrived yesterday. We are about two miles below our last permanent camp, about four below the mouth of the Rosebud, and nearly opposite the point where our three men were killed in May, which, after one of the number, is now called by us Raymeyer Butte. As we are likely to remain here some time, the camp was laid out with great care, and what with the level ground and its growth of fine grass, presents a very neat appearance. Just above is a dense thicket of willow and cotton-wood, and scattered about the camp are a few cotton-wood trees, which combine with the camp and the river to form a very pleasing and picturesque view. Many of our camps in the march down and up the Yellowstone have been of the same agreeable character, and have imparted quite a charm to this warlike jaunt of ours.

Thursday, 15. Thompson's and Wheelan's companies left today on a five days' scout up the Yellowstone to see whether the Indians are keeping south of the river. Six Crows accompany them. The remainder of the cavalry moved up and joined on the lower side of our camp. A mail was sent with Thompson's command, and will be forwarded by couriers from the point where they turn back.

Friday, 16. Today the Crows discovered a heavy smoke across and up the river, apparently on O'Fallon Creek. It suggested a world of speculation, one of the theories being that a Sioux village had been attacked and destroyed either by Custer or Crook. It means more likely that the Sioux are moving in that direction and accidently set the grass on fire. Toward evening it died out. Some rain today.

Saturday, 17. Still lying in camp, waiting for the steamboat which is daily expected. Orders were today issued to company commanders to keep three days' cooked rations constantly on hand and to be prepared to cross the river at once upon the arrival of the boat. The cavalry pickets thought they saw two men on the bluffs across the river, but the Crows who were on the lookout saw nothing, and it is probable that the pickets were mistaken.

Sunday, 18. This afternoon Major Reno, with six companies of the 7th Cavalry, appeared at the mouth of the Rosebud and went into camp. General Gibbon went up opposite the camp and held a conversation with him by means of signal flags and afterwards communicated with him by letter through two Crows, who swam the river for that purpose. Reno's command had scouted up Powder River,[37] then crossed

[37] For the details of this scout, one of the most controversial matters connected with the Battle of the Little Big Horn, see Edgar I. Stewart and

to the Rosebud, and scouted down the latter stream, meeting with no Sioux but finding recent traces of a large village at the place I discovered it on the twenty-seventh of May. Mitch Bouyer, our guide, who had been detached to accompany Reno, counted 360 lodge fires, and estimated that there were enough beside to make the number of lodges about 400 hundred. The lodges had been arranged in nine circles within supporting distance of each other, within which the Indians evidently secured their horses at night, showing that they considered an attack not unlikely and were prepared for it. A well-defined trail led from the site of the village across the plain toward the Little Big Horn, and it is now thought that the Indians will be found upon that stream.

Monday, 19. Major Reno's command broke camp this morning and moved down the river after supplies. Towards evening Thompson's and Wheelan's companies returned, having scouted up to the mouth of the Big Horn. They met no Sioux and saw no sign of them on this side, and but little on the other. The Crow village which some weeks ago was on the Big Horn seems to have disappeared from that country—another indication that the Sioux are heading in that direction. It is pretty well demonstrated that they have no intention of crossing to the north side of the Yellowstone, as they would not have passed so high up the stream for that purpose.

Tuesday, 20. Captain Freeman has been ordered to march up the river tomorrow with Companies E, H, and K of the infantry battalion to bridge creeks and otherwise put the road in order. He will take ten days' rations and will be accompanied by six Crow scouts.

Major E. S. Luce, "The Reno Scout," in *Montana, the Magazine of Western History*, Vol. X, No. 3 (July, 1960), 22–29. The diary of Dr. James M. DeWolf, on which the previous article is based, was edited by Major Luce and published in *North Dakota History*, Vol. XXV, Nos. 2 and 3 (April–July, 1958).—E. I. S.

Wednesday, June 21. Captain Freeman's command got off about six A. M. Soon afterward the steamboat was reported in sight, whereupon orders were issued to prepare to move. At 8 A. M. the boat arrived, having on board General Terry and staff and Captain Baker's company of the 6th Infantry. We were ordered to march at once to Fort Pease, and got off at 9:30 A. M., Captain Ball commanding, General Gibbon and Major Brisbin having gone on board the boat, intending to rejoin us at some point in advance.

Custer with the entire 7th Cavalry was reported near at hand, and soon after we started, he appeared in view on the table-land across the river, marching toward the Rosebud.[38] The steamboat met him at the mouth of that stream, when he drew rations for his command for sixteen days and struck out up the Rosebud with the design of following up the trail found by Major Reno. Prior to his departure a conference took place on the boat between Generals Terry, Gibbon, and himself with reference to a combined movement between the two columns in the neighborhood of the Sioux village about the same time and assist each other in the attack, it is understood that if Custer arrives first, he is at liberty to attack at once if he deems prudent. We have little hope of being in at the death, as Custer will undoubtedly exert himself to the utmost to get there first and win all the laurels for himself and his regiment. He is provided with Indian scouts, but from the superior knowledge possessed by the Crows of the country he is to traverse, it was decided to furnish him with a part of ours, and I was directed to make a detail for that purpose. I selected my six best men, and they joined him at the mouth of the Rosebud. Our guide, Mitch Bouyer, accompanies him

---

[38] For a description of the disparity between the two commands, see Edward J. McClernand, "With the Indians and Buffalo in Montana," *Cavalry Journal*, No. 36 (January–April, 1927), 16.—E. I. S.

also. This leaves us wholly without a guide, while Custer has one of the very best that the country affords. Surely he is being afforded every facility to make a successful pursuit.

We marched eighteen miles and camped at 7:05 P.M. on the Yellowstone, a short distance below the mouth of the Great Porcupine, having passed Captain Freeman's command in camp at the spring a couple miles back. As we passed, Capt. Ball ordered him to move down and join us—a very unwelcome order to Captain Freeman's men, who were comfortably settled for the night. The camp was barely formed when a terrible gale arose, followed by a storm of hailstones as large as walnuts. The herd showed a strong disposition to stampede, and it required great exertions to prevent them from doing so. The hailstones diminished in size as the storm continued and soon turned to rain; but the shower was of short duration, and before dark the sky partially cleared and the sun treated us to a gorgeous display in the west.

Thursday, 22. During the night Lieutenant Low, 20th Infantry joined us with his battery of three Gatling guns. They belonged to Custer's column but were detached therefrom under the impression that they might impede his march.

It rained considerable during the night, and as a consequence the road in the valley was very muddy. The cavalry battalion separated from us this morning, under orders to push on to Fort Pease as rapidly as possible, the infantry following as fast as it can. Low's battery goes with the cavalry. The cavalry started at 6 A.M., and we followed at 7, soon passing the cavalry, whose train got stuck in the mud. The two battalions crossed the Great Porcupine at different points, the infantry after crossing taking at once to the bench lands, while the cavalry continued on up the valley. As a consequence, the order of things was getting rapidly inverted, the infantry going to Fort Pease first, and glorying in their ability to outmarch the D. P.'s; but at this juncture Captain Freeman chivalrously halted his column and let the cavalry go by. We marched twenty-nine miles and made a pleasant camp on the bank of the Yellowstone at 5:30 P.M., the cavalry camping in sight above us, having been able to gain only a mile and a half. We expected the steamboat to pass us today, but it has not appeared.

Throughout the campaign the General has allowed neither drums nor bugles to sound, believing they might be the means of communicating information to the enemy. As a consequence strength of lung has been a very essential qualification in our battalion adjutants, who, when the time for roll-calls or beginning the day's march arrives, must post themselves in a conspicuous position and bawl out the command loud enough to be heard all over the camp: "Form your companies!" Fortunately the gentlemen officiating in this capacity in their respective battalions have not been wanting in this regard; but still the cheerful rattle and toot of the proscribed instruments has been greatly missed, so much so that one of our officers who met some of the companies of Custer's command was heard to declare that, favorable as was the general impression they produced on his mind, there was nothing that delighted him more than the refrain of their bugles. Our cavalry comrades have been particularly restless under this prohibition, and it was observed today that no sooner did they cut loose from us than they began to sound their bugles with hearty good will. So much did the buglers glory in their new-found freedom and the mellow notes they poured forth that they exerted themselves fit to crack their throats, and repeated the calls far more freely than was necessary for the mere information of the command. And candor compels me to say that, notwithstanding its dulcet capabilities, the voice of our adjutant shouting his old familiar cry of "Form your companies!" did not begin to produce as pleasant an effect upon the ear as the "sonorous metal" of the cavalry "braying martial sounds."

Friday, 23. The reveille of the cavalry bugles came sweetly to the ear this morning across the intervening space. Broke camp at 6:05 A. M., and soon came up with the cavalry, who were still in camp but saddling up. Their train had pulled out and had the road ahead of us, and our train was unable to overhaul it, although our teamsters were stimulated to do their best by the promise of a considerable purse that some of our frolicsome infantrymen made up in the interests of a race. The day was excessively hot and there was a deal of dust, making the marching quite disagreeable. The cavalry kept well in advance of us all day, in fact passed quite out of sight. Lieutenant Doane and "Muggins" Taylor, who were scouting ahead, saw several Sioux on the bluffs across the river, and also about a thousand buffalo running at full speed. A considerable number of the latter crossed the river and were intercepted by Lieutenant Doane's party, who killed several of them. The cavalry supplied themselves liberally with the meat and had the kindness to butcher some also for the infantry, Lieutenant Doane remaining in person to notify us of it and point it out as we came up. We were greatly in need of it, having had very little fresh meat for a considerable period, but Lieutenant Jacobs, our quartermaster, with unaccountable obstinacy and disregard of the men's welfare, objected to the train halting for the few minutes necessary to take it on, and Captain Freeman yielded the point and passed it by. So we marched into camp and supped on bacon, instead of the excellent buffalo steaks we might have had.

At 5:30 P. M. we camped on the bank of the Yellowstone about a mile below Fort Pease, having marched twenty-two miles. The cavalry had gone on and camped about two miles above the fort. The steamboat was sighted a few miles below this evening, and will probably be up early tomorrow.

Saturday, 24. The steamer passed our camp at 4:30 A.M., and moved on up to the camp of the cavalry. At 6 A.M. we broke camp and joined the cavalry, and soon afterward the whole command, except Captain Kirtland's Company (B), were ordered to prepare to march at once with eight days' rations and a pack train. The cavalry companies were assigned six and the infantry companies four pack-mules each, the train and camp equipage being left behind guarded by Company B.

About 11 A.M., twelve Crow scouts were carried over the river by the steamer to scout up Tullock's Fork, with orders to proceed until they found a Sioux village on a recent trail. About noon the boat began to ferry over the remainder of the command, the cavalry going first in three trips, the Gatling battery, my detachment, and part of the infantry on the fourth trip, and the remainder of the infantry on the fifth, all being over about 4 P.M. My detachment then passed to the front, and the march began up the Big Horn, just below the mouth of which our landing had been effected. Arriving at Tullock's Fork, a tributary of the Big Horn, we turned up its valley and at 6 P.M. camped about a mile above its mouth at the foot of a perpendicular wall of rock, having marched about five miles since leaving the boat. General Terry and staff came up and joined us about an hour later; they are provided with common tents—a small wedge-shaped tent—while the command bivouacs in the open air. General Gibbon has been quite sick and is still on the boat, but is expected to join tomorrow.

Just before dark the twelve Crows came whooping down the valley, behaving in such extravagant fashion that all expected some startling disclosure; but it turned out that they had merely seen, six miles up the valley, a buffalo that had been recently wounded with arrows. Their orders had been to go ahead until they found a village, and now after wasting eight hours in advancing ten miles, they return with this paltry piece of news. It was amusing to listen to the comments of some of the "pilgrims"[39] as to the importance to be attached to this momentous intelligence. It really amounted to nothing, as the buffalo might have been wounded by a small war or scouting party a hundred miles from any camp; but the "pilgrims" saw in it positive evidence of the near vicinity of the village we are after. The Crows know better than to attach any such importance to it, but were glad of any subterfuge to return to the protection of the command.

We are now fairly en route to the Indian village, which is supposed to be on the Little Big Horn. It is undoubtedly a large one, and should Custer's command and ours unite, we, too, will have a large force numbering all told about one thousand men, armed with the splendid breech-loading Springfield rifles and carbines, caliber forty-five, and strengthened by the presence of Low's battery of three Gatling guns. Should we come to blows it will be one of the biggest Indian battles ever fought on this continent, and the most decisive in its results, for such a force as we shall have if united will be invincible, and the utter destruction of the Indian village, and overthrow of Sioux power will be the certain result. There is not much glory in Indian wars, but it will be worth while to have been present at such an affair as this.

The "Far West" will, if practicable, ascend the Big Horn as far as the mouth of the Little Big Horn, and there await tidings from us.

Sunday, 25. At 4 A.M., in compliance with orders, I sent

[39] A name given in the West to newcomers who are ignorant of the ways of the country and unused to its rough experiences.

six Crows up Tullock's Fork, and half an hour later followed with the remainder of the Crows and my detachment. At 5:30 A. M. the command broke camp and marched two miles up Tullock's Fork and then turned off to the right into the hills, expecting to find a comparatively level table-land leading to the Little Big Horn. Meantime I had ascended the stream nine miles, when I halted to await some indication that I was being followed by the command, and after a long delay was overtaken by a squad of cavalry sent to notify me of the change of route. I soon rejoined, taking a short cut across the hills, and found the command involved in a labyrinth of bald hills and deep, precipitous ravines completely destitute of water. The men had emptied their canteens of the wretched alkali water they started with and were parched with thirst as well as greatly fatigued with clambering over such ground. A worse route could not have been chosen, but destitute of a guide as we are, it is not to be wondered that we entangled ourselves in such a mesh of physical obstacles.

While the command struggled on toward the Big Horn as the nearest point of escape, I executed an order given me by General Terry to scout to a distant ridge on the left of our line of march, from which it was thought the Little Big Horn might be seen and possibly an Indian camp. Reaching the ridge after an exceedingly toilsome march of eight miles over a very rough country, I found myself confronted by another ridge a few miles farther on that completely obstructed the view. Having been ordered not to pass the first ridge, I turned back and overtook the infantry battalion at 6:50 P. M., just as they were going into camp in the valley of the Big Horn. There I learned that some of the Crows who had gone up Tullock's Fork in the morning had discovered a smoke in the direction of the Little Big Horn, which was thought to indicate the presence of the Sioux village, and the cavalry and

Gatling battery, accompanied by General Terry, were pushing on with a view of getting as near it as possible tonight. The infantry, which had already marched twenty-three miles, were to remain in camp for the night and follow in the morning

I joined the cavalry with my detachment, orders having been left for me to that effect. A brisk rain set in toward evening, and continued to fall in successive showers through the first half of the night. Darkness overtook us still pushing on up the Big Horn, and though the march had been difficult by day, it was doubly so in the darkness of the night. The cavalry officers who scouted up the Big Horn last April were acting as guides, for want of better, and, as their knowledge of the country was far from profound, we were continually encountering serious obstacles to our march—now a precipitous hillside, now a deep ravine. Occasionally, as the head of the column was checked, we would find ourselves closed up in a dense mass, and again, where the path grew narrow, we would stretch out in an attenuated thread, the men in the rear racing desperately after those in front [so as] not to lose sight of them in the gloom and be left without a clue to the direction they had taken. Every now and then a long halt was made, as an avenue of escape was sought from some topographical net in which we had become involved.

There was great danger at times, when the column stretched out to unusual length, that it would become broken and leave us scattered over the country in a dozen bewildered fragments, and once the cry did go up: "The battery is missing!" A halt was made, and after some racing and hallooing the missing guns were set right again, having lost the human thread and so wandered a mile or so out of the way. At another time some of the cavalry went astray and lost half an hour getting back to us.

At length, after hours of such toil, getting out of one difficulty only to plunge at once into another, the head of the column came plump on the brink of a precipice at whose foot swept the roaring waters of the Big Horn. The water gleamed in front 150 feet below, and to the right hand and to the left the ground broke off into a steep declivity, down which nothing could be seen but forbidding gloom. Our cavalry guides were wholly bewildered, and everybody was tired out, and dripping with wet, and impatient to get somewhere and rest. When General Terry saw the walls of Fort Fisher before him, he knew what to do. He threw his battalions against them, and carried them by storm, and gained a glorious victory and won a star; but when he saw to what a pass we had now come and reflected that every step we took seemed only to render our situation more perplexing, he appeared uncertain and irresolute. For several minutes we sat our horses, looking by turn at the water and into the black ravines, when I ventured to suggest to the General that we trust ourselves to the guidance of Little Face, one of my Crow scouts who had roamed this country as a boy fifty years ago and had previously assured me that he knew every foot of it. Little Face was called up, said he could guide us to a good camping-ground, was accepted as a guide, and led off in the dark with as much confidence as though he was in the full light of day. The aimless, profitless scrambling was over; he conducted us by an easy route a mile or two to the left, where we found ourselves in a commodious valley with water enough in its little channel to suffice for drinking purposes. There was not much grass for the animals, but it was the best we could do without going several miles farther, and so about midnight we halted, unsaddled, and threw our weary forms down on the ground for a little rest, the cavalry having marched about thirty-five miles and my detachment, in consequence of its diversions from the main column, about fifty-five.

Monday, 26. Major Brisbin, who in General Gibbon's absence commands the column, roused me up this morning at daylight and ordered me out on a scout at once, not allowing my men to get breakfast. As I had traveled some twenty miles farther yesterday than anybody else, so that my horses were tired and my men hungry, it struck me as rather rough treatment. I was too much vexed to hurry much, and did not get off till 4 A. M., having sent six Crows ahead half an hour earlier. My orders were to scout to the Little Big Horn, looking out for Sioux sign and sending back word of any important discoveries. Having advanced about three miles, we entered a valley cut by a dry creek, and here came upon the fresh tracks of four ponies. As we entered the ravine, we had seen a heavy smoke rising in our front, apparently fifteen or twenty miles away, and I at once concluded we were approaching the Sioux village and that the trail had been made by a party of scouts therefrom.

Sending back a written report of the discovery, I took the trail of the four supposed Sioux in the hope of catching them in the Big Horn valley, toward which the trail led and where we thought they might have camped, as there was no convenient way of leaving the valley into which they had gone except that by which they had entered it.

At the distance of less than two miles the trail struck the river, and we found that they had there crossed, leaving behind a horse and several articles of personal equipment, indicating that they had fled in great haste. An examination of the articles disclosed to our great surprise that they belonged to some of the Crows whom I had furnished to General Custer at the mouth of the Rosebud, which rendered it probable that the supposed Sioux were some of our own scouts who had for some reason left Custer's command and were returning to the Crow agency. While speculating upon the circumstance, three men were discovered on the opposite side of the Big Horn about two miles away, apparently watching our movements. We at once signaled to them with blankets that we were friends, for a long time to no purpose, but when we were about to give up and seek some other method of communicating with them, they responded by kindling a fire that sent up a small column of smoke, indicating that they had seen signals and trusted our assurances. We gathered wet sage-brush and assured them with a similar smoke, and soon afterwards they came down to the river and talked across the stream with Little Face and one or two more of the scouts who went down to meet them. While the interview went on, I kept the remainder of the detachment on the bluffs. Presently our Indians turned back and, as they came, shouted out at the top of their voices a doleful series of cries and wails that the interpreter, Bravo, explained was a song of mourning for the dead. That it boded some misfortune there was no doubt; and when they came up, shedding copious tears and appearing pictures of misery, it was evident that the occasion was of no common sort. Little Face in particular wept with a bitterness of anguish such as I have rarely seen. For awhile he could not speak, but at last composed himself and told his story in a choking voice, broken with frequent sobs. As he proceeded, the Crows one by one broke off from the group of listeners and going aside a little distance sat down alone, weeping and chanting that dreadful mourning song, and rocking their bodies to and fro. They were the first listeners to the horrid story of the Custer massacre, and, outside of the relatives and personal friends of the fallen, there were none in this whole horrified nation of forty millions of people to whom the tidings brought greater grief. The three men over the river were in truth a portion of the six scouts furnished to General Custer from my detachment; and this is the story they had told to Little Face:

After Custer left the mouth of the Rosebud, he had followed the Indian trail and yesterday struck the village on the Little Big Horn, the Sioux warriors letting him get close to the village and then sallying forth in overwhelming numbers to meet him, defeating his command, and destroying all but a small portion, who had been driven into the hills and surrounded by the Sioux, where the Crows had left them fighting desperately. The corpses of Custer's men were strewn all over the country, and it was probable before this that the last one was killed, as it was impossible for the party who had taken refuge in the hills to hold out long, for the Sioux immensely outnumbered them and were attacking them in dense masses on all sides. Of the six Crows who had gone with Custer, two—White Swan and Half Yellow Face—were killed, and another—Curly—was missing and probably also killed. The fighting had occurred at the point where the smoke was then rising in our front. It was a terrible, terrible story, so different from the outcome we had hoped for this campaign, and I no longer wondered at the demonstrative sorrow of the Crows. My men listened to it with eager interest, betrayed none of the emotion of the Crows, but looking at each other with white faces in pained silence, too full of the dreadful recital to utter a word. Did we doubt the tale? I could not; there was an undefined vague something about it, unlooked for though it was, that commanded assent, and the most I could do was to hope that in the terror of the three fugitives from the fatal field their account of the disaster was somewhat overdrawn. But that there had been a disaster—a terrible disaster—I felt assured.

It was my duty to report it to General Terry, and being a

matter of such importance I resolved to make the report in person, as I now saw the head of the column appear over the ridge a couple of miles away. I therefore rode back until I met the command, which was halted just before I came up, and narrated to the General the ghastly details as I had received them from Little Face. He was surrounded by his staff and accompanied by General Gibbon, who had that morning joined [them], and for a moment there were blank faces and silent tongues and no doubt heavy hearts in that group, just as there had been among the auditors of Little Face at its rehearsal by him. But presently the voice of doubt and scorning was raised, the story was sneered at, such a catastrophe it was asserted was wholly improbable, nay, impossible; if a battle had been fought, which was condescendingly admitted might have happened, then Custer was victorious, and these three Crows were dastards who had fled without awaiting the result and told this story to excuse their cowardice. General Terry took no part in these criticisms, but sat on his horse silent and thoughtful, biting his lower lip and looking to me as though he by no means shared in the wholesale skepticism of the flippant members of his staff. My imagination was busy supplying to my mind his train of thought, and it ran like this: "The story may not be true, when we have only to push on according to the original plan. It may be true, and it then becomes our duty to hasten to the rescue of the miserable remnant of Custer's command surrounded on the hills. If the savages have been able to destroy Custer's noble six hundred, what can we hope to accomplish with our paltry four? But we will do the best we can and rescue the wretched survivors or ourselves perish in the attempt." And as though it were the seal of authenticity to this bold attempt to divine the workings of his mind, he cried, "Forward!" and once more the column was in motion toward the foe. My duty there was done, and taking a rapid gait, I soon gained my proper distance in front as advance guard.

The infantry had remained in camp last night twelve miles back and at 5 A. M. resumed the march, coming up with the cavalry toward noon, having been greatly delayed by the pack-train. The whole column then advanced together, and having crossed the dry creek, where I now found the trail, and the rugged divide separating it from the Little Big Horn, entered the valley of that stream. The heavy smoke was now continually in view, and notwithstanding the stiffened limbs of the infantry, in consequence of their hard march yesterday, the prospect of an early arrival at the village and a brush with the Indians imparted a wonderful animation to their movements and urged them on at a rapid gait. After passing up the valley a few miles, the column crossed to the left bank and soon afterward halted to allow the men to rest and make coffee.

The three Crows who had escaped from Custer's battlefield promised to recross the Big Horn and rejoin the command, provided some of their comrades waited for them, and partly on this account and partly to allow them time to recover from their grief, I permitted all the Crows to remain behind when the column passed the point where we had received news of Custer's overthrow. Bravo, the interpreter, stayed with them, and as he was frightened nearly out of his wits by the unfortunate tidings and anxious to avoid going on,[40] he no sooner saw us fairly out of the way than he exerted himself to induce the Crows to abandon the expedition, representing to them that some of our officers had said we no

---

[40] Lieutenant Bradley was apparently prejudiced against this man. As the Journal makes clear, Bravo had rendered efficient and valuable service. In this case the criticism of him was unjustified as he was merely being realistic in the face of disaster.—E. I. S.

longer wanted their services. Several of the best Crows were opposed to such a measure, but Bravo, aided by some of the malcontents among them, carried the point against such, and the whole body were seen by some of the officers at the rear of the column to mount and gallop away together. They recrossed the river and proceeded straight to the Crow agency.

During our afternoon rest, citizens Bostwick and Taylor were sent forward by different routes toward the village to reconnoiter and communicate with Custer should he prove to be in possession. While they were still absent and after we had rested about two hours, the column was again, at 5 P. M., put in march up the valley, my detachment in advance. After advancing about two miles, I discovered several ponies on my left front, towards the river, and taking Corporal Abbott with me, moved over to investigate. They proved to be five in number, evidently estrays from the village, and taking possession of them, I sent them back to the column. Not long afterward I discovered three or four mounted men about two miles in advance, and at once deployed my detachment as skirmishers; and soon afterward Bostwick came into view down the valley galloping at full speed. As he came up, he paused long enough to say that he had proceeded cautiously up the valley for several miles until all at once he came plump on a considerable body of Indians. Not caring to cultivate their acquaintance nearer, he turned short about and retreated at the best speed of his horse.

It was now sufficiently evident that we had Indians in our front, and the column advanced slowly in fighting order, the Gatling battery and three companies of cavalry in column on the right, four companies of infantry in column on the left, and one company of infantry and the pack-mules in the center —a part of the infantry company at the head and part at the rear of the packs. Generals Terry and Gibbon with their staffs rode at the head of the column, Lieutenant Roe with his company of cavalry being advanced half a mile or so on the bluffs to the right, while I moved abreast of him on the left up the valley, passing through the timber that grew in occasional clumps along the stream.

As we advanced, I continually saw Indians up the valley and on the bluffs to the right, riding about singly and in groups of two, three, half a dozen, and more. Once they appeared to the number of seventy-five or a hundred on a distant hill, and not long afterwards several rifle shots rang out from the bluffs where Roe was advancing, and a few shots were exchanged by the Indians and a few of our eager men who pushed to the front. One circumstance caused me a good deal of disquietude, and that was that the Indians were evidently massing in the timber at a narrow place in the valley, with the apparent intention of resisting at that point our further advance. Squad after squad of mounted savages galloped down the slope of the hills into this grove until I estimated that not less than a hundred had entered it after we came into view, and how many other hundreds might already have been there or entered by some other way could only be conjectured. As I had this timber to go through with my detachment, it was not pleasant to think of the storm of bullets that would undoubtedly be hurled into our faces as we rode up to its dark border or of the painted hundreds that would rise suddenly on all sides of us, as we got fairly entangled within its recess, and cut off the whole of us in a moment. I have been in several engagements and participated in several charges upon intrenched positions, but in my whole career as a soldier never did anything call for so much nerve as the riding slowly up with eleven men, half a mile from the rest of the column, on this body of ambushed warriors. My men sat their saddles with pale faces but closed lips with stern determination, expecting in a few minutes more to be shot down, but resolved not to flinch though the cost were death.

Meanwhile Lieutenant Roe was advancing on the bluffs and from his elevated position could see a long line of moving dark objects defiling across the prairie from the Little Big Horn toward the Big Horn, as if the village were in motion, retreating before us. But between him and them was a numerous body of warriors, estimated by some observers as high as three hundred men. Those nearest him appeared to be clothed in blue uniforms, and carried guidons, forming in line, breaking into column, and otherwise maneuvering like a body of cavalry. Under the impression that they might be members of Custer's command a sergeant and three men were sent forward several hundred yards, and when well advanced, the sergeant left his men and approached them along to within hailing distance; but upon calling out to them was quickly undeceived as to their character by receiving a volley in response that caused him to retire hastily. About this time Taylor returned from his attempt to reach the village (beleaguered cavalrymen), having, like Bostwick, encountered Indians but not escaping without being fired upon.

My detachment was now drawing near the timber in which the Indians were ambushed, and we were nerving ourselves for the expected annihilation when the column halted, and I, too, halted, something like a quarter of a mile from the timber. At this moment several horses emerged from the timber and came directly toward us, some of the men asserting that they bore riders, but it was now twilight and I could not tell with certainty. Bostwick and Will Logan saw these horses from the bluffs and resolved to attempt their capture. The horses had stopped about halfway between my line and the timber, but Bostwick and Will boldly passed in the rear and drove them toward my line, having been close under the guns of the ambushed Sioux, who could easily have picked them off had they chosen to fire. But probably expecting soon to get my detachment in range, they forebore to do so, and the venturesome fellows got off safe and conducted their booty to the camp—four good Indian ponies.

Lieutenant Burnett soon rode up to inform me that camp was forming, and that I was to remain where I was until the cavalry companies ceased watering and then join the command. This was very welcome intelligence, indeed, as it saved us from riding into the dreaded ambush and seemed like a gift to us of our lives. The cavalry companies were watering a few hundred yards in our rear and finished soon after dark, and we then returned, finding the command bivouacked in the valley midway between the stream and the bluffs and about half a mile from each.[41] No fires were allowed, and we lay upon our arms, arranged in a square, but with a very weak face indeed down the river, that side, I believe, being occupied by only a guard of twenty-odd men. The animals were secured within the square. The halt was made at 9 P.M., the infantry having marched thirty miles, the remainder of the command about eighteen. The steamboat is working its way up the Big Horn, having touched this morning at the point where the infantry camped last night. General Gibbon remained with it up to that time and then came on and joined the command early in the day.

Before retiring, the officers assembled in groups and talked over the events of the day. I found that a majority of the infantry officers placed confidence in the report brought by

41 This camp was on the site of the present Crow agency, about thirteen miles south of present Hardin, Montana. The center of the camp was about where the schoolhouse now stands.—E. I. S.

the Crows of Custer's overthrow, and were prepared for unpleasant disclosures upon the morrow. Some of the cavalry
officers also shared in this conviction, but the majority of
them and about all of the staff were wholly skeptical and still
had faith that Custer had been victorious if he had fought
at all. So obstinate is human nature in some of its manifesta-
tions that there were actually men in the command who lay
down to sleep that night in the firm conviction, notwithstanding all the disclosures of the day, that there was not an Indian
in our front and that the men seen were members of Custer's
command. They could explain ingeniously every circumstance that had a contrary look, and to argue with them was
worse than useless. Some of the cavalry officers had a theory
that a great mistake was committed in not sending them forward with a dash, when the Indians were first discovered,
to hack the enemy in infinitesimal mince-meat. They still,
months later, adhere to this position, and I therefore take this
occasion to give my testimony that such a proceeding would
have been in the highest degree absurd. Had they been sent,
they had the spirit to go forward gallantly, but there were
Indians enough in the timber and on the hills before them,
in chosen positions of great strength, to have cut them all to
pieces and driven them back in ruinous disorder. From subsequent examination of the ground I am convinced that there
were not less than a thousand of these ambushed savages,
with plenty more to co-operate with them, and not only would
they have easily defeated the cavalry, but they would have
given our whole command a desperate fight had we advanced
that evening another mile. Their village was retreating, and
they were there to cover it, and it was only for lack of an hour
or two more of daylight that we did not come upon them in
force and prove once more the terrific gallantry with which

they can fight under such an incitement as the salvation of their all.

Tuesday, June 27.[42]

[42] At the time of the commencement of his final campaign (that under Colonel John Gibbon against the Nez Percé Indians in 1877), Lieutenant Bradley was engaged, during such leisure moments as were at his command, in the preparation of manuscript for a book which he intended to publish. He had gathered to that end a considerable amount of valuable historical, military, and other matter, of which not the least interesting is the above record of the Sioux campaign of 1876. During the interval between these two campaigns, his original notes that had been taken in camp and upon the march were enlarged upon and the manuscript of military operations against the Sioux in which he had been a participant was prepared to this point, when the memoir stops thus abruptly at the very outskirts of Little Big Horn's fatal field. This is much to be regretted, as it is certain that Mr. Bradley's account of the scenes and incidents of Custer's last brave fight and Reno's defensive rally would have been of considerable interest and of historical and military value.

It is evident that at this point in his work of compilation, the soldier was called to enter upon the expedition against the hostile Nez Percés, from which he was destined never to return, and that he laid down his pen with the expectation of taking it up once again at some future and more peaceful period.—W. E. S.

Force Participating in the Little Big Horn Battle, Together with the Killed and Wounded[1]

Mr. Will Logan, son of Captain Wm. Logan who was killed at the battle of the Big Hole, August, 1877, has in his possession a piece of Indian parchment found on Custer's battlefield shortly after the fight. Captain Logan's company clerk made out on this piece of parchment a list of killed and wounded in this engagement, together with a brief statement relative thereto, and it is through the kindness of Mr. Logan, now living at Elkhorn, Montana, that an exact copy is here given. It is to be regretted that no date is given when the list was made out, but it must have been soon after the battle.

[1] This tabulation was printed at the end of the Bradley Journal in *Contributions to the Historical Society of Montana*, II (1896), 225–26.—E. I. S.

True account of killed and wounded in fight with Sioux Indians on the 25th and 26th June, 1876, on Little Big Horn River, Montana T'y.

Present before action, as follows:

Field and Staff, Commissioned _____ 6
Line, Commissioned _____ 25

Total Commissioned _____ 31
Enlisted Men _____585
Citizens _____ 8
Scouts, Indians Ries* _____ 6
Crow Indians _____ 25

624

Total Com., enlisted etc., etc. _____655
Missing after action _____332
Total remaining after action _____323

Killed and wounded as follows:
Killed with General Custer, as follows:

Officers _____ 13
Enlisted men _____191
Citizens _____ 4

Total killed with General Custer _____208
Killed with Major Reno, as follows:

Officers _____ 3
Enlisted men _____ 48
Citizens, scouts, etc. _____ 5

Total _____ 56
Wounded with Major Reno _____ 59
Died of wounds since _____ 8

Total killed _____260†
Total remaining wounded _____ 51

* Rees.
† Wrong; 264, not counting those who died of wounds afterward—author of footnote not identified.

Force Participating in the Little Big Horn Battle

General Terry and Colonel Gibbon with six companies, 7th Infantry and four companies, 2nd Cavalry, crossed Yellowstone River, June 24, 1876, with intention to assist General Custer in attacking a large Sioux village on Little Big Horn River, M. T., but General Custer did not wait for said command and attacked the village, five companies charging, one company with pack-train and six companies with Major Reno on the opposite end of the village. General Custer with his five companies was cut down entirely; the company with packs joined Reno, who with the seven companies was obliged to retreat to the hills, where the Indians held him and cut him off from water for thirty-six hours until their scouts (Sioux) discovered the approach of General Terry's command, when they abandoned their village and left during the night, leaving considerable plunder after them, also some ponies. General Terry's command arrived on the battle-ground, June 27, at about 6 A. M.; remained there and buried all dead and took care of wounded; started for steamer "Far West" June 29th, and met near mouth of Little Big Horn, June 30th; put wounded on board and started back for old camp on Yellowstone near mouth of Big Horn where the command arrived July 2, 1876.

According to Captain E. S. Godfrey, 7th Cavalry, the killed and wounded of the entire command was respectively 255 and 52. (See *Century Magazine*, January, 1892.)—H. S. W.

Note: See "An Indian Massacre," Page 32[1]

FORT ATKINSON, July 3, 1823.

Dear Sir:—How painful for me to tell, and you to hear, of the barbarity of the Indians. . . .

"The defeat of General Ashley by the A'Ricarees, and departure of the troops to his relief, had scarcely gone to you when an express arrived announcing the defeat by the Blackfoot Indians, near the Yellowstone River, of the Missouri Fur-Company's Yellowstone or mountain expedition, commanded by Messrs. Jones & Immell, both of whom, with five of the men, are among the slain. All of their property, to the amount of $15,000, fell into the hands of the enemy. . . .

The express goes on to state, "that many circumstances (of which I will be apprised in a few days) have transpired to

1 From *Contributions to the H. S. M.*, II (1896), 226–27. The page on which "An Indian Massacre" appears in that volume is 154.

induce the belief that the British traders (Hudson's Bay Company) are exciting the Indians against us, either to drive us from that quarter, or reap, with the Indians, the fruits of our labor." . . .

They furnish them with the instrument of hell and a passport to heaven—the instrument of death and a passport to our bosoms.

Immell had great experience of the Indian character, but, poor fellow, with a British passport, at last they deceived him, and he fell a victim to his own credulity, and his scalp, with those of his murdered comrades, is now bleeding on its way to some of the Hudson establishments. . . .

I am at this moment interrupted by the arrival of an express from the military expedition, with a letter from Dr. Pilcher, whom you know is at the head of the Missouri Fur-Company on this river, in which he says, "I have but a moment to write. I met an express from the Mandans, bringing me the very unpleasant news—the flower of my business is gone. My mountaineers have been defeated, and the chiefs of the party both slain; the party were attacked by three or four hundred Blackfoot Indians, in a position on the Yellowstone River, where nothing but defeat could be expected. Jones and Immell and five men were killed. The former, it is said, fought most desperately. Jones killed two Indians, and in drawing his pistol to kill a third, he received two spears in his breast. Immell was in front; he killed one Indian and was cut to pieces. I think we lost at least $15,000. I will write you more fully between this and the Sioux.

Jones was a gentleman of cleverness. He was for several years a resident of St. Louis, where he has numerous friends to deplore his loss. Immell has been a long time on this river, first an officer in the United States army, since an Indian trader of some distinction; in some respects he was an extraordinary man; he was brave, uncommonly large, and of great muscular strength; when timely apprised of his danger, a host within himself. The express left the military expedition on the first instant, when all was well. With great respect, your most obedient servant,

BEN. O'FALLON,[2]

U. S. Agent for Indian Affairs.

GENERAL WILLIAM CLARK,

Supt. Indian Affairs, St. Louis.

[2] Benjamin O'Fallon was for many years an Indian agent of the United States. He was an honest, courageous, and careful officer, who possessed great influence over the various tribes with whom he came in contact and was of great service in aiding the government in many treaties. His memory is perpetuated in the West by O'Fallon's Bluff, on the Platte River in Nebraska, and O'Fallon's Creek in Montana, near Glendive.—W. E. S.

Note: Manuel Lisa; See "The Missouri Fur Company," Page 18[1]

MANUEL LISA WAS A SPANIARD by birth who had moved to St. Louis from New Orleans only a few years before the transfer of the "Louisiana Purchase" to the United States. He was a man of kind and upright character, of undoubted business ability and indomitable energy, who possessed a thorough knowledge of the aboriginal peculiarities and characteristics and who had great influence with the Indians with whom he was thrown, being liberal and just in his dealings with them. Furthermore, he was of that venturesome and independent spirit which found its chiefest delight in overcoming the dangers and enduring the hardships incident to the venturesome life of the trader within that *terra incognita* of ninety years ago that then stretched over all the vast watershed of the Missouri River.

[1] From *Contributions to the H. S. M.*, II (1896), 228. The page on which "The Missouri Fur Company" appears in that volume is 146.

Together with Captain William Clark and ten others, in 1808, he helped to inaugurate and establish the Missouri Fur Company, and was thereafter its head and front for a number of years. His methods of trade with the Indians may best be explained by an abstract from one of his letters, which will also serve to explain the man:

"First, I put into my operations great activity. I go a great distance while some are considering whether they will go to-day or to-morrow. I impose upon myself great privations. Ten months of the year I am buried in the depths of a forest at a great distance from my own house. I appear as a benefactor, not as a pillager of the Indian. . . . Beside, my blacksmiths work incessantly for them, charging nothing, I lend them traps, only demanding a preference in their trade. My establishments are the refuge of the weak, and of the old men no longer able to follow their lodges; and by these means I have acquired the confidence and friendship of the natives and the consequent choice of their trade."

He was twice married; his first wife[2] having, with her daughter, been a prisoner among the Indians until rescued by General William Henry Harrison. A widow, her husband having been killed at the time of her capture, Manuel Lisa in pity of her friendless condition married her, placed the mother and daughter in affluence in a comfortable home and treated them with the greatest affection and consideration.

He left no children, and at his death, which occurred near St. Louis, his property passed to the children of his brother. —W. E. S.

2 From the context it would seem that this should read "his second wife." —E. I. S.

Lieutenant Bradley's Letter
To the Helena Herald, July 25, 1876

To the Editor of the Herald:—
Helena, M. T., July 25th, 1875 [*sic*].

In the presence of so great a disaster as that which overtook the regular troops on the Little Horn,[1] and the consequent excited state of the public mind and its eagerness to get hold of every detail, however minute, of that unfortunate affair, it is to be expected that many stories of a sensational character having no foundation in truth would obtain currency in the newspapers and credence with the public. Of such a character is that now going the rounds of the press, to the effect that the Sioux had removed Custer's heart from his body and danced around it, a story related upon the

[1] At this time the names Little Horn and Little Big Horn were both used for the stream.—E. I. S.

authority of one Rain-in-the-Face, a Sioux chief who participated in the fight and afterward returned to his Agency.[2] Of the same character, also, is the sweeping statement as to the general shocking mutilation of the bodies of the soldiers who fell on that occasion. The bare truth is painful enough to the relatives and friends of these unfortunate men without the cruel and gratuitous exaggeration of their grief that must come from the belief that they had been horribly mutilated after death. It therefore seems to me worthwhile that these stories should receive emphatic contradiction, and being in a position to make such a denial I address you this letter with that object.

In my capacity as Commander of the Scouts, accompanying General Gibbon's column, I was usually in the advance of all his movements, and chanced to be upon the morning of the 27th of June, when the column was moving upon the supposed Indian village in the Little Horn valley. I was scouting the hills some two or three miles to the left of the column upon the opposite bank of the river from that traversed by the column itself, when the body of a horse attracted our attention to the field of Custer's fight, and hastening in that direction the appalling sight was revealed to us of his entire command in the embrace of death. This was the first discovery of the field, and the first hasty count made of the slain, resulting in the finding of the 197 bodies reported by General Terry. Later in the day I was sent to guide Colonel Benton [Benteen][3] of the 7th Cavalry, to the field, and was a witness to his recognition of the remains of Custer. Two other officers of the regiment were also present, and joined in their identi-

[2] Rain-in-the-Face was not a chief, and there is doubt whether he even participated in the battle.—E. I. S.

[3] Frederick W. Benteen, the senior captain of the regiment and the most outspoken critic of Custer among the officers.—E. I. S.

fication; and as all had known him well in life, they could not
be mistaken and the body so identified was wholly unmuti-
lated. Even the wounds that caused his death were scarcely
discoverable (though the body was entirely naked) so much
so that when I afterwards asked the gentlemen whom I accompanied whether they had observed his wounds they were
forced to say that they had not.

Probably never did a hero who had fallen upon the field
of battle appear so much to have died a natural death. His
expression was rather that of a man who had fallen asleep
and enjoyed peaceful dreams than that of one who had met
his death amid such fearful scenes as that field had witnessed,
the features being wholly without ghastliness or any impress
of fear, horror, or despair. He had died as he had lived—a
hero—and excited the remark of those who had known him
and saw him there, "You could almost imagine him standing
before you!" Such was Custer at the time of his burial, on
the 28th of June, three days after the fight in which he had
fallen, and I hope this assurance will dispose of the horrible
tale of the mutilation and desecration of his remains.

Of the 206 bodies buried on the field, there were very few
that I did not see, and beyond scalping, in possibly a majority
of cases, there was little mutilation. Many of the bodies were
not even scalped, and in the comparatively few cases of dis-
figuration, it appeared to me the result rather of a blow with
a knife, hatchet or war club to finish a wounded man, than
a deliberate mutilation. Many of Custer's men must have
been disabled with wounds during the fight, and when the
savages gained possession of the field such would probably
be mainly killed in the manner indicated. The bodies were
nearly all stripped, but it is an error to say that Kellogg, the
correspondent, was the only one that escaped this treatment.
I saw several entirely clothed, half a dozen at least, who, with

Kellogg, appeared to owe this immunity to the fact that they had fallen some distance from the field of battle, so that the Indians had not cared to go to them, or had overlooked them when the plundering took place. The real mutilation occurred in the case of Reno's men, who had fallen near the village. These had been visited by the squaws and children, and in some instances the bodies were frightfully butchered. Fortunately not many were exposed to such a fate. Custer's field was some distance from the village, and appears not to have been visited by these hags, which probably explains the exemption from mutilation of those who had fallen there.

Yours truly

JAMES H. BRADLEY, *First Lieut.*

7th Inft.[4]

[4] This letter added by the present editor, Edgar I. Stewart.

Index

[Since there are references to Lieutenant Bradley, the Crow Indians, and the Yellowstone River on almost every page, only the more important items have been indexed under those headings.]

Index

Index